How To Do
All Things
Your Use of Divine Power

by

EL MORYA/MARK AGE

Published for
THE HIERARCHAL BOARD
and the
UNIVERSITY OF LIFE
by
MARK-AGE
Pioneer, Tennessee, USA

Revision and expansion of Mark-Age
periodicals of same title published 1965.

Cover design by Phillel.
Front: Line drawing is by Owen Morrison, depicting
materialization of divine power as and through El Morya.
Back: Photo of El Morya/Mark, 1966.

E-mail: iamnation@aol.com
Website: http://www.thenewearth.org/markage.html

ISBN 978-0-912322-65-0
Library of Congress Control Number: 2017915478

FIRST EDITION—1970
SECOND EDITION—1973
THIRD EDITION—1981
FOURTH EDITION—1988
FIFTH EDITION—2018

Manufactured in the United States of America
by Sterling Pierce Co., Inc., East Rockaway, New York

CONTENTS

Names and New Age Terms

▲

ENCODED SPELLINGS

Several times in his text, El Morya/Mark intentionally spells *dis-ease* with a hyphen. Metaphysically, the encoded spelling connotes not only "disease" in the usual sense but also a lack of ease or harmony or balance. (See also *disease* in Glossary.)

Similarly, on page 126, *dis-order* indicates a lack of order; that is, a condition out of perfect order or alignment.

In "Co-operate with God," on page 137, and also elsewhere in the text, *co-operate* means "to operate together" with Spirit or Divine Mind to perform actions of creative manifestation.

How To Do All Things

All Things

Your Use of Divine Power

MARK-AGE

_____

HERALDING SECOND COMING

Mark-Age, Inc. is a nonprofit spiritual-educational organization, founded in 1960. Our teachings are based on the interdimensional communications of Nada-Yolanda, a prophet for the New Age and the Second Coming (see pages 5–6). Coexecutive directors are Phillel (Philip J. Jacobs) and Robert H. Knapp, M.D.

The primary purpose of Mark-Age is to externalize on Earth the Hierarchal Board (spiritual government of our solar system) in preparation for the Second Coming in its dual meaning: the second coming of each one's I Am Self, expressed through the mortal personality; and the Second Coming of Sananda/Jesus the Christ, Prince of Earth, in his resurrected, etheric, light body in the beginning decades of the new millennium.

We are in the long-prophesied Latter Days, the War of Armageddon between good and evil, a period of planetary cleansing when the signs or marks of the age point to a new spiritual dimension of love, peace and brotherhood to come. This is the harvest time, the transition cycle between the ending of the old, materialistic age and the New Age of Aquarius, now dawning.

I AM NATION

Mark-Age has been commissioned by the Hierarchal Board (i.e., ascended masters and angelic guardians) to implant a prototype of spiritual government on Earth, the I Am Nation.

The I Am Nation is a government of, for and by the I Am Selves of all people on Earth. Regardless of race, religion, gender, age, nationality or spiritual-group affiliation, everyone is a potential I Am Nation citizen.

The I Am Nation is not a political government, but is a spiritual congregation of all souls who seek to serve God, first and foremost, and the I Am Selves of all people on Earth.

FIVE DIVISIONS

The physical, legal vehicles for the externalization of the I Am Nation are the five divisions of Mark-Age, Inc.

I AM NATION NEWS: Media outlet for publishing news, information, education and guidelines for the linking of light workers and groups in preparation for the Second Coming and the New Age of Aquarius. Also, the name of our bimonthly newsletter.

I AM NETWORK OF LIGHT: Interdimensional and international network of individuals and groups who coordinate in weekly meditation broadcasts. Prayers, visualizations and projections of spiritual power help uplift humanity for the Second Coming. Since 1972, more than 2,275 audiocassette broadcasts have been recorded.

UNIVERSITY OF LIFE: Mass educational program featuring textbooks, self-study courses, booklets, audio and video recordings, and other materials teaching spiritual mastery of life. Divided into twelve schools covering all essential aspects of life on Earth.

HEALING HAVEN: Presentation of the best holistic and orthodox information, techniques and research for the spiritual healing of humanity in mind, body and soul. Teaches how to establish health and harmony of the four lower bodies (mental, emotional, astral, physical) so as to aid the anchoring of the resurrected, immortal, light body through the mortal personality and form.

CENTERS OF LIGHT: Local focuses of two or more individuals who gather to learn spiritual knowledge and to demonstrate the divine commandment *Love God and Love One Another.* "Where two or more are gathered, there I Am."

> *For a listing of Mark-Age books, booklets, courses, audio and video recordings, and subscriptions, please send for our free catalog.*

El Morya/Mark Age (Charles Boyd Gentzel) was born on November 11, 1922, in Youngstown, Ohio, to Mary Yaskalko and Charles A. Gentzel. He was the oldest in a family of one sister and two brothers. He graduated in 1940 from Clarks Summit–Clarks Green High School near Scranton, Pennsylvania, and planned a career as a research chemist. From 1941 to 1943 he worked as a chemical laboratory technician for a brass company in Bridgeport, Connecticut.

From 1943 to 1946, during World War II, he served in the United States Army in Belgium, France and Germany as a master sergeant in the Quartermaster Corps. He received an honorable discharge.

After the war, he attended Cornell University in Ithaca, New York. Graduating with honorable distinction in 1949, he received an A.B. degree in Chemistry (with a minor in Economics).

EL MORYA/MARK, 1966

Mark-Age as an organization name was received intuitively by Mark at Easter 1949. As he contemplated not going into graduate study in chemistry, he was considering the business alternatives, having had such a background prior to college. The decision was made at that time to start such a firm after graduation in June.

Although the name of the work and the Latter-Day period was given from the higher planes, it consciously was derived from the projected nature of the business. Mark-Age apparently stood for *Mark*eting *Age*nts. The Mark-Age slogan was to be: *The best of the new, direct to you.* There were to be three major divisions of this international sales organization, bringing new products via independent salesmen or agents to homes, businesses, industries.

Mark left Ithaca–location of Cornell University–for Rochester, New York, in June 1949. He registered Mark-Age as an assumed business there on August 12, 1949. But since this really was not the intended nature of Mark-Age and as there was a recession at the time, there never was any actual business conducted.

After a brief trip to Los Angeles, California, in February 1952, in an attempt to locate there, he returned to New York and started a sales business in Auburn. The name used was Mark-Age, registered in Auburn on June 17, 1952. This business was discontinued in 1954.

Then he moved to Syracuse, New York, to operate an employment agency he had purchased. A business recession forced the closure of this in 1958. He remained there until February 1959.

Leaving Syracuse, he went again to Los Angeles in another attempt to locate there, but returned in a few weeks. He stayed at his mother's home in central Pennsylvania until finances permitted him to go forth again to try to found Mark-Age.

But now he knew part of the spiritual intent of Mark-Age. This began in 1955, after becoming aware of practical metaphysics when he read the books of Thomas Troward and sought a church which followed these ideas. He found it in the Unity church in Syracuse and in the publications of the Unity School of Christianity.

With this spiritual awakening, and its following urgent and intensive metaphysical study and practical application, soon came a deeper understanding of what Mark-Age really was.

At Easter 1956, Mark received intuitively the first spiritual insight into the actual purpose of Mark-Age. He set down then the *Mark-Age Manifesto* and the twelve departments. But still he had no conscious awareness of a spiritual Hierarchy, let alone life on other planets and a hierarchal plan and program. In 1957–58 he inspirationally wrote *How To Do All Things.*

Mark saw Mark-Age then as a long-range program to bring all on Earth into Christ awareness through Christ teachings and demonstrations, much as Jesus of Nazareth had done. But most of the program was seen to be from the inner planes or the spiritual-mental level, from where much lifting of all on Earth could be done without their conscious knowledge, understanding and participation.

With this in mind had Mark set out in March 1959 to begin Mark-Age in southern California. He went from Syracuse to Los Angeles via Miami, Florida, staying there four days. But again he

NADA-YOLANDA & EL MORYA/MARK, 1962

was unable to remain in California, for something within would not let him do so.

While waiting in Pennsylvania to start again, he bought a Miami newspaper in the summer of 1959, surveying the employment possibilities there, should he go to California or elsewhere via Miami in the winter. Therein he found an advertisement for a counselor in an employment agency in Miami. He wrote to the Miami firm, on the chance it might provide at least a start. The reply was merely to the effect that if he were to go there, he should visit the office to see about the position.

He left Clarks Summit, Pennsylvania, five miles north of Scranton, in mid-November 1959, arriving in Miami the day before Thanksgiving. He went to the agency office, only to learn that the owner, who had written to him, would not be back until after Thanksgiving. So, he went back on December 1st and discussed the opening with Miss Pauline Sharpe, known now to us as Nada-Yolanda.

Noting on his application form under "hobbies" that he was interested in metaphysics, Yolanda inquired further about this topic. It was then that he gave Yolanda the printed *Manifesto* and the twelve departments of Mark-Age. He took her to her first Unity church service on December 10th. He gave her the manuscript of *How To Do All Things* to read on December 13th. Metaphysical discussions and meditations were a daily feature during this period of becoming acquainted.

In the late 1950s, Nada-Yolanda (1925–2005) had had a sudden spiritual awakening and had begun to develop her elementary spiritual powers (ESP). She experienced contacts with ascended masters from the higher planes, who opened her as a psychic communications channel. Her initial receivings were via automatic writing, then later via conscious mental telepathy. After meeting Mark, she shared her automatic writings with him, and he pronounced them authentic.

On February 21, 1960, following high Self guidance, Mark and Yolanda made the covenant with Sananda/Jesus the Christ to form the Mark-Age organization for the Second Coming program.

Since 1960, Mark-Age has published books, booklets, courses, magazines, newsletters, and audio and video recordings for an international membership of individuals, churches, schools, universities and independent study groups who network globally to bring a new level of spiritual consciousness to planet Earth.

In addition to El Morya/Mark's *How To Do All Things*, Nada-Yolanda's books are considered the preeminent texts internationally for spiritual Self-development. Some of her best-known titles are: *MAPP* to Aquarius: *Mark Age Period and Program, Evolution of Man, Angels and Man, Visitors From Other Planets, Birth of the Light Body, Facts of Life, Prophecies: 2000–4000 A.D., Metamorphosis: from Mortal to Immortal, Cosmic Laws, Contacts from the Fourth Dimension, Life in Our Solar System, Anchoring the Light Body on Earth, Autobiography of a Prophet,* and a metaphysical novella, *My Divine Love.*

After Mark's transition to the higher realms in 1981, Yolanda became executive director and president of Mark-Age. She remained our primary communications channel until her own transition in 2005, at age eighty. From the inner planes, both Nada-Yolanda and El Morya/Mark continue to guide and to inspire the Mark-Age United Staff and all receptive I Am Nation citizens.

▲

INTRODUCTION

How To Do All Things is a textbook explaining methods whereby one can achieve more spiritual understanding and greater use of divine power. Written in an easy-to-understand manner, it is of value to both beginning and advanced students of mind. The techniques are those used in spiritual works of Mark-Age since 1956 and thus are thoroughly proven.

The book was written initially in 1957–58, first revisions were made in 1964, a softcover edition was printed in 1965, final revision was completed in 1969, and the hardcover edition was published in 1970. It was prepared for mass distribution at the time when spiritual demonstrations throughout the world in the Latter-Day period and program would instigate a desire within mass consciousness for explanations and instructions. Since 1981, subsequent editions, including this fifth one, have been published in trade paperback format.

Section I consists of six chapters of basic explanatory material concerning spiritual principles. Section II sets forth one hundred spiritual truths as examples of basic realities to be substituted for some of the erroneous ideas which have limited man and have tended to prevent him from attaining his true spiritual nature and heritage here on Earth.

Section III explains and demonstrates fifty examples of how to do specific things by use of the principles given in the first section. Section IV was channeled through Nada-Yolanda on September 26, 1968, by El Morya, who is the Christ Self of Mark Age, author of this book. Thus in actuality El Morya is the real author, having given through the mortal consciousness of Mark Age the ideas set forth in *How To Do All Things.*

The photograph of Mark on the following page was taken in 1960 when he and Nada-Yolanda made the covenant to begin the public functions of Mark-Age to serve the Hierarchal Board.

EL MORYA/MARK AGE
November 11, 1922 — April 24, 1981

I. YOUR USE OF DIVINE POWER

1. SEVEN STEPS FOR GAINING FULL USE OF DIVINE POWER

FIRST: OF YOURSELF YOU CAN DO NOTHING

This book obviously could not attempt to give specific instructions on how to do everything in particular. Huge libraries of books could not do that, not only because there are so many things man has learned how to do but also because there are so many he has not learned to do yet. Then why the title?

The important matter is not learning how to do particular things but rather learning certain basic facts about universal laws in general. This general understanding will enable one to learn how to accomplish easily whatever particular things he wishes.

The first step in this process of learning how to do all things will seem strange at first reading, but the explanation immediately follows. It is of the utmost importance that this first point is fully understood, for without it there would be no use trying to understand the rest.

In order to do all things, you must first know that you can do nothing! That is exactly right; you never have been able to do anything and you never will be able to do anything. Once you understand this, why it is so, you have the key to accomplishing all things you desire, providing your wishes are proper.

The addition of two words to this first point will serve to amplify and to explain it. The statement then becomes: of yourself you can do nothing. This may sound nonsensical but a little guided analysis will show the statement to be completely true.

No matter what one believes, actually he can do absolutely nothing. This is because man is not just a physical body with a brain but is a spirit with mind and body. The body, although part of man, is his fleshly home in this world. It is, or at least is meant to be, at his command so he may function properly in this plane of existence.

Consider even such a basic part of life as moving one's body. Can you move any part of your body? No. What actually happens is that your body moves at your command. Do you know what your body does in order to move a finger when you so desire? If you do not know how to do the actual work involved in moving the body, how could you claim you did the moving?

The only work you do to effect any movement of your body is to think what you want to do. This necessarily does not include the automatic functions of your body, since it is not even necessary for you to think about them in order for them to be performed. Once you have issued an order, by wishing a certain movement to take place, and providing your body is functioning normally and the movement has been learned, it is done. You do not know how this mental command of yours has been relayed through the brain in the necessary electrical, chemical and physical sequences to cause the movement. Nor is it necessary that you know the steps. But a little contemplation should convince you that you do not and cannot make the movement yourself. All you can do, and all you need do, is command.

Once you understand your inability even to move your body, it is easy to carry the analysis further and to see that if you cannot move your body you certainly cannot move anything else. When you have understood that you cannot do anything in a physical sense, but rather that you cause things to be done, you are ready for the second point.

This is the all-important point to understand, but you first must know the preceding point. It is not a principle that sometimes works one way and sometimes another, but it is always the same. It is the only power, and therefore it cannot be used in all things if you look for more than one power. However, learning that all power is one, you then can learn to use it for specific purposes. This is how you will learn to do, or how to have done, all things.

SECOND: ALL IS DONE BY SPIRIT

This second point is that all things are done by the only power or moving force that exists. This power is Spirit. It is Spirit that moves your body as you wish. It is Spirit that is the only force, whether It works electrically, chemically, physically or in any other way.

You are a conscious identity or personality that thinks. Spirit as moving force is at your disposal to accomplish what you desire. You do the thinking and commanding, Spirit performs the work. This is the meaning of the scripture: "Not by might, nor by power, but by my Spirit, says the Lord of hosts." The plan is as simple as that.

But it is this very simplicity which causes man so much difficulty. First he must learn how to think properly so Spirit, which acts as an impersonal force, will not accomplish what he really does not want, even though actually, through misunderstanding, he has asked for it. Also, he must learn what Spirit cannot do: go against universal or divine laws. Since Spirit is the only power, It cannot work against Itself. When man attempts to make It do so, man experiences trouble.

In addition to this, when man clearly perceives that there is but one power, he will be able to study the one force and, learning Its principles, apply them to the study and use of all particular manifestations of force. Then he will know all forces as phases of but one force and will not hamper himself by many gods instead of just the one God.

This is exactly what some mathematicians and scientists have been seeking: a unified field force; proving electricity, magnetism and gravity, the three recognized as basic at that time, actually to be just three phases of one elementary force. The next and final step is full recognition that this elementary force is Spirit. Metaphysicians of philosophy and religion have stated this clearly for thousands of years.

Getting back to you as an individual, it is necessary that you recognize Spirit as the only motivating force and that It has been placed at your disposal by divine decree. But only to a limited extent, until you learn to command properly. It would be well here to define *command* as meaning a request, or speaking the word, to initiate action.

11

We can, for the purpose of analysis, divide into three degrees the extent to which Spirit as force is put at our disposal. First are the automatic functions of the body and of nature in general. Without going into detail, many of the actions in the body and in nature are not as automatic or uncontrollable as most people believe. These can be governed so as to function properly. Second are the functions man has learned to control, again both in the body and in nature. Third are the functions he has not been able to control yet, either through lack of understanding or not knowing of their existence. Man consciously cannot employ a force properly if he is unaware of it or does not understand it to some degree. That is precisely the purpose of this book: to call attention to one force acting as all forces or power and to learn enough about this primary force, Spirit, to enable us to use It as God intends.

THIRD: KNOW YOU ARE A SPIRITUAL BEING

This leads us to the third point in our study of how to do all things. It is to learn our relationship to this force. You must be able to understand yourself as a spiritual being, thus placing Spirit as force at your disposal as an integral part of your spiritual nature. This force is yours to use to a certain extent in what is called the physical, to a much greater extent in what is referred to as the mental, and to an infinite manner in the spiritual realm. Or briefly, It is yours to use to the extent you are able to perceive and to understand It and Its capabilities. Since It is divine, Its capabilities are infinite.

It acts for you to the extent you recognize your authority, or privilege, in the proper manner. It is to the potential usage of Spirit as force that the Holy Bible refers when stating that man is made in the image and likeness of God. *Image* means according to God's idea of man. *Likeness* means similar to God's nature, with the use of His powers. Spirit as force is His motivating or creating power.

FOURTH: LIVE UP TO YOUR SPIRITUAL NATURE

The fourth point follows closely the third, in that once we have understood our relationship to God, we must act the part. It is necessary that one act according to his inherent spiritual nature before he can be entrusted with other than minor use of Spirit as force. How to do so will be found later in this book. This step also includes knowing what to decree, what action to take, in the sense of what we should do. Again, knowing this in general, we can more easily see how to apply it to specific cases.

FIFTH: LEARN TO DECREE PROPERLY

The fifth point is learning how to decree, or learning how to initiate action which will be carried out for us by Spirit. Included in both the fourth and fifth studies is seeing how we actually decree, and receive, things we do not want; also how we receive things because we do not decree otherwise. It is so true, in this sense too, that ignorance of the law is no excuse; one can suffer from lack of doing something as well as from doing something. This is a vitally important part of our instruction in how to do, by having done, all things.

SIXTH: BE RECEPTIVE TO GOD'S IDEAS

The sixth point of such accomplishment is learning how to achieve always greater use of this force. We wish to learn more of the higher uses of our body in this world. We are impelled to learn more of God's plans for us and all the rest of His creation so we may bring forth His ideas into manifestation. Just as the wonders of the first half of the twentieth century were not envisioned by most men, so are there infinite wonders yet in store for us. But we, merging the infinite and the finite, must learn how to have these works brought forth through our initiation of action. As we learn more about general principles, we are able to apply such knowledge to specific purposes. We must learn how to do this for ourselves and for others. As one achieves in this sixth study, he enters into an infinite wonderland which as yet has been explored but little by few on Earth; a land which has no boundaries, limitations or end of exciting and glorious discoveries.

SEVENTH: ATTAIN YOUR INHERENT PERFECTION

The seventh point is the logical and inevitable concluding study in how to do all things: functioning in eternal consciousness unhampered by any physical limitation. As one acquires this understanding, he attains complete and eternal control over his bodies, thus enabling him to function perfectly anywhere forever. He never lays aside his physical body unless he so wishes, and then he can take it up again or change it at his will. This too is done by Spirit according to one's understanding.

Thus are finished the seven studies leading to complete entry into the spiritual realm, where one truly can do all things. The seventh study, as well as those following, are not included in the scope of this book. However, all who are able to complete and to understand the first three of these studies have become truly aware of their eternal existence. At this stage all fears are gone and one begins to live in the eternal now.

SUMMARY OF SEVEN STEPS

In summary and for handy reference, the seven points or studies in learning how to do all things are as follows:

1. You of yourself can do nothing in a physical sense.

2. Spirit is the only power or force which can do anything. You decree; Spirit does. Therefore, you can do all things, which are proper within divine law, by having them done for you by Spirit. Your doing is thinking; Spirit's doing is acting.

3. Your relationship to Spirit as motivating power is that of a spiritual being who, made in the image and likeness of God, has uses of power as does God. This force is the only power; therefore, It is the accomplishing agent for God and all His creations.

4. The degree of responsiveness of Spirit to your requests for action depends on the degree to which you live up to your inherent spiritual nature. You will not be entrusted with any great use of the power of Spirit if you seek to go contrary to divine law. That is impossible.

5. Your ability to initiate action to be carried out by Spirit depends

on knowing how to decree properly. This includes learning how to stop improper decreeing and how to prevent others' beliefs and decrees from affecting you.

6. You must learn how to become receptive to receiving God's ideas and how to initiate the action that will bring these heavenly treasures into physical manifestation, the earth. This entails continual increase of understanding to help not only ourselves, but others also, to achievement of inherent spiritual perfection.

7. Your last step in overcoming all limitations of this world is the attainment of the perfection God decreed for you. This is the complete control of your consciousness and body to the extent that you use them as you wish in eternal living. Now are finished the mortal limitations, now are increased the spiritual glories.

▲

2. THE REAL POWER

YOU CANNOT DO THE WORK

You can do all things because of yourself you can do nothing. Since this statement seems contradictory and because it is so important as the starting point in learning to accomplish whatsoever we would and should, let us examine it in more detail. Even though now you may see how it is true, it would be well to enter this discussion with us, for, being such a basic premise, it so often is forgotten temporarily by many who have become advanced students. It is often a good practice to review essentials, especially when one seems to have strayed off the path of proper demonstration.

As precedence in making such statements, we have the best of authority. The most outstanding is Christ Jesus of Nazareth. He clearly and simply stated this truth by saying, "I do nothing of myself, but the Father abiding in me, He does the works." Would it not be wise to heed such a user of Spirit? Yet Jesus did many wonderful things. But it was in the sense of decreeing or requesting that it be done, and it was done.

What a marvelous plan God has established for us. We have no need to concern ourselves with most of the functions of our bodies. It is not necessary to decide consciously which muscles move any part of the body. Imagine what such necessity would mean, for example, in walking. There is no need for us to work in the digestion of food. Who could decide all the processes and movements of the body, let alone do the work, in converting food into energy after it enters the mouth? It is not necessary that we concern ourselves with the automatic functions of the body. This frees us for the more important work of thinking, learning how to initiate action, initiating it and enjoying the results.

Some may be thinking that we really are doing this work, because it is being done by the subconscious. In a sense that is true, but the subconscious is actually another phase of our complete conscious-

16

ness, and each of those phases is dependent on the one and only power for action. This particular analysis can be carried far into the deep mysteries of being, but that is only for greatly advanced students. It is the study of the Trinity of God, and also of man; how the three are really one but in practice work as three. So, if any advanced student should be alarmed about the statement that we can do nothing, but Spirit does all, let him rest assured that the unity of Trinity is understood. However, we are here concerned with action and works, not merely contemplation.

PERFECTION OF BODY

The question may arise as to why, if Spirit does all the work in the body, there ever should be such a thing as malfunction or other undesirable results. The answers are: we often interfere in various ways, we may not recognize Spirit as the acting agent, or we fail to realize Spirit would cause proper functioning if we so asked. As for interference, this can be in the nature of doing what we should not, of thinking what we should not or of neglecting to think properly for ourselves. In not recognizing Spirit as the intelligent force managing the body, we may try to figure out how things should be done and believe it must be done our way. One who truly recognizes Spirit as the manager of his body never experiences anything but bodily perfection. In such a person nothing could go wrong, because he permits intelligent Spirit to do the work It fully understands.

For one who may have anything functioning improperly, let him now recognize Spirit as the power that knows what to do and how to do it, and let him ask Spirit to take full charge and to manifest perfection of body. It will be done. But do not take back this permission by doubting the ability of Spirit or by trying to tell It how to work.

As for medicine or other external help in regaining normalcy, Spirit does not need them. If you use them, do so with spiritual studies and techniques. Basically, recognize that many fully master these first three studies. However, know that many medicines are gifts of God to aid those who still basically believe themselves to be physical or mental beings alone rather than spiritual, which includes the others. But since they are used by those who still are limited in the understanding of their own true nature, the medicines thereby are also limited. Have courage, though, for all eventually shall understand in full.

To summarize this section so far: all that is necessary for your body to function properly at all times is to recognize intelligent Spirit as the force that produces, maintains and moves your body. Then, and this is important, give Spirit full authority to do all of this. If you do not see the results immediately, or even over a period of time, do not become impatient or cancel your recognition and grant of authority. The fault will not be that of Spirit but will be due to your interfering in some way, probably quite unknown to you consciously. Further study or consultation with one who has gone ahead will reveal and will remove the difficulty.

SPIRIT IS PRIME MOVER OF ALL CREATION

Once you have recognized Spirit as the moving agent of your body, you are ready to see It as the prime mover of all creation. Much study is needed to learn enough of Spirit and Its many workings for you to be able to have It do the infinite things you will learn to have done by your proper requests. Such study in detail is not the purpose of this book, but there is already much good instruction available and more to come. Do not concern yourself now with locating them. When you are ready for them and desire them, you will have them.

By now it should be much easier to realize that you actually do no physical work yourself. This does not mean your body does not get tired during physical work. It does mean the real you is the thinking or knowing you, while your body is your means of expression in this world. Learn to think of Spirit as doing the physical work, and the resulting strength and fitness of your body will astound you. Try it before you begin some strenuous work or play. Ask Spirit to do the work, and thank It for doing so. If any who read this would scoff, theirs is the loss. You who try it will know it works for you, while they only would know it does not for them.

The next step is to visualize Spirit as performing all body movements easily. This is not to suggest you are to expect to be able to do great physical feats at once. If such is desired, extensive training is necessary spiritually, mentally and physically. But your body not only will function properly at all times, also it will be in good condition. You will not be tired all the time and your body tone will be excellent. You will reach the state where you usually are unaware of your body from the health standpoint. When you are aware of it, it will be in the joyousness of a vibrantly healthy body that is serving you perfectly, and that always will. It is a wonderful feeling.

PROTECTION

From here your contemplation goes outside your body. Would you like to be assured of no accidents in your travel by car? All you need do is ask Spirit to do the driving through you, or whoever is at the wheel. Of course, you must do your part too. But you will be guided and will be warned of any danger in time to avoid it. Or, when this is not feasible, it will be taken care of for you. Also, your actions in time of danger will be far quicker than your reactions normally would permit. Many drivers who give Spirit this task have had apparently miraculous escapes for themselves and others.

This also applies to protection from other motorists or their cars. It further applies to the working of your car, for Spirit is also the force that moves all parts of the car. Do not think this eliminates the necessity of having a safe and properly working car, for we now are talking about protection, not elimination of common sense and responsibility.

This protection applies equally well to all forms of travel. Before beginning any trip ask for, and believe you are receiving, the protection of Spirit. Give thanks for the safe journey in advance. Then do what you should and leave supreme responsibility with Spirit. In this manner have you learned to do another important thing: travel safely. Just as you learned how to have a continuously healthy body, you also have learned how to do your traveling: by letting Spirit do it for you. Simple? Yes, it is.

You have noticed in this section we have been dealing in some measure with the first three points rather than just the first. This has been done so there will be no confusion or dismay caused when someone states what is wrong or must not be done but does not go on to say what is right or must be done. However, this procedure is progressive in that the second point has been considered less than the first so far, and the third even less than the second.

Now that you are more familiar with the first point, it will drop further into the background until you seldom will remember it consciously. Nevertheless, it has become part of your thinking, one of the automatic parts. The same will be true of each following point. By the time you have completed the seventh study, most of your actions automatically will have taken all the acquired understanding into account. You already are familiar with this process in the workings of the body which you have learned since infancy.

DAILY TASKS

You are now ready to do all of your normal daily tasks easier and better. How? Right; by knowing that Spirit does the work, not you. This analysis of the work you used to think you of yourself did can be a fascinating study. Inasmuch as this book is not attempting to achieve the impossible, doing your thinking for you, there will be only a few more examples, to give you a pattern to follow and to reveal in some measure the scope. Then you can enjoy many hours of personal exploration. You would find it profitable to do some of this before beginning the next chapter. Future rereading will stimulate new observations each time. Just a few helpful words here: you will gain little if you do not try them. As you do apply them, you not only will enjoy their fruits but you also will open the door to achieve more.

Are you a housewife? Try doing your housework as many others have: by seeing Spirit as the worker. When you can fully grasp this, you will have attained to an understanding that will not be mentioned further for now. But by visualizing Spirit as the working force, you will be surprised at how even the most dreaded tasks assume a new pleasure. You no longer will regard necessary chores in terms of boring time, but you will take pleasure in doing them; of course, you know we really should say, pleasure in having them done. Pleasant surprises in this connection will come when you discover that while doing these tasks, rather than fretting by thinking of your need to do them, you will be free instead to entertain happy thoughts. For it will become less and less a case of your both thinking and working, and more and more a case of your thinking while Spirit does the work. Whether in housework or other work, you will gain more hours of pleasure and instructive thoughts each day.

SPIRIT AS WORKING POWER

Before continuing with examples, it would be well to say a few words about Spirit as working power. It is not in the least a presumption or a sacrilege on the part of anyone to ask Spirit to work for him. In our introduction of this reality we noted that, since we of ourselves can do nothing, there must be some working force or forces that do work, since work is done. Since there is only one power, God, all work must be done by God. We are speaking here of that phase of the Trinity of God which we are calling Spirit, power, force, working agent and other names. This range of names is deliberate, not only to indicate somewhat the range of Spirit as force but also to show that the name we use is not as important as knowing what we are naming.

Since it is the nature of Spirit as power to do all the work in the universes, we do not and could not offend or tire It. And since it is our nature as God's manifestations to speak the words that initiate the prime mover, we do only what we should when we properly and abundantly make use of It. The scriptures tell us to let whoever is greatest among us serve us. Who is greatest among us, if not God? Only, here we are considering the moving force, Spirit, as the phase of Divine Trinity that serves us as power. Nevertheless, consider anyone who truly loves; does he not long to be able to help and to serve? Who can love as God loves?

Finally, one sees through the fallacy of failing sources of power when he can see Spirit as the only real power behind all other forms of what man calls power sources. There never has been and never will be a time when man has no power supply. There has been no real occasion to worry about dwindling supplies of fuel wood, coal, oil, gas, uranium or any others. As man evolves he discovers new sources, each more powerful. Also, each is less physical in nature. Man has gone from solids to liquids to gases to atoms. His final and all-powerful step will be to recognize Spirit as the only power. Then he will be shown how to make use of this power without intricate machinery for conversion to energy.

Are you a factory worker, a professional man or woman, a clerical worker, a laborer or anyone whose work is all or partly physical? Or are you an athlete, a musician, an artist or anyone whose efforts require highly skilled body movements? That is correct: Spirit does the work, not you. Of course, you must do these things enough to acquire the necessary familiarization of movement and you must have developed such other things as skill. But instead of trying to force such practice yourself, acknowledge Spirit as the mover. This leaves you free to concern your thinking with the skill itself rather than with the work of expressing it.

However, do not make the mistake of thinking Spirit will do more for you than for another, for Spirit does not favor anyone over another. It only seems so because some make better use of this power provided by Spirit. In other words, it is the understanding of anything and the use you make of Spirit as force that differentiates, not Spirit Itself.

ANALYZE YOUR PHYSICAL EFFORTS

This should suffice to give you the manner of looking at all things requiring physical effort. Now would be a good time to set aside the book for a while and to apply the analysis to all of your physical activities. Another time you can devote to the activities of others you know, and then to work in general. On other occasions you should devote meditation to those things you want to do, such as learning to drive a car, to swim, to play at a sport, to play an instrument and so on and on. You will begin to look forward with joyful anticipation to cooperating with Spirit in all activities. You then will have expanded your how-to-do's so as to include a vast number of physical activities. Why not all physical activities? Not only would you require additional skills, knowledge and understanding but you have neither

22

the time nor interest for all things now. But others will have these where you do not, so all may be served.

This would seem to take care of the physical aspects of work and how you can have all things done. But such is far from the case. There are many activities that seem to be outside man's range of control. These are classified in general as nature and would include such things as weather, rivers, land, and activities of minerals, plants and animals. Much has been done by man's initiative action in all these and many others, but such works are permitted only those who have fitted themselves, and who consequently have been given the understanding, to have such things accomplished. You either have known of or will hear, will see or will do some of these.

"The works I do shall he do also; and greater than these shall he do, because I go unto my Father." You too can go to your Father God within and about you. There in thought you will gain more understanding, and then greater use, of Spirit. "You shall also decree a thing, and it shall be established unto you."

APPLICABLE TO ALL REALMS

This has led us to consider what you may have been asking already. Does this work by Spirit at your request apply only to the physical? Or does it apply to the mental, and perhaps spiritual, realm as well? The answer is that it applies to all of these. Since this activator is Spirit, It necessarily must include functioning on all planes. You eventually will understand that even these three realms are a trinity that is one. That is, there are not actually three distinct and separate realms, only three phases of one realm. But we need not go into this advanced subject to enable us to achieve the application of the material in this book.

Neither do we want to consider the mental and spiritual levels in this section, for our study of them in this respect more properly belongs in later sections. We will consider one more topic here after briefly mentioning what the later studies will cover. Since Spirit is God, or one of the Holy Trinity if you so wish to consider It, Spirit is one with all that God is. Thus we see that we can turn to Spirit for guidance, information and understanding. Indeed, Spirit is the only source of all real wisdom. He is the source of all true ideas. He knows the solution to all problems we may face. And He is always instantly and easily available. We only need know this and learn how to contact Him.

You already are on the way if you have done nothing else than apply what you have read so far in this book. You shall go much further by the time you have finished, have understood and have applied all that is contained herein. It is not enough alone, but it will help, for it is inherent in the nature of this book.

MANAGING YOUR AFFAIRS

You also may enlist the services of Spirit in managing your affairs. Many people and firms employ a manager or a staff to handle their affairs. Yet the perfect manager is ever willing to help in whatever proper way you wish. Naturally, this does not mean you will be able to eliminate competent assistants in all of your affairs. Rather, it is intended to point out that it is no more an infringement on your personal rights to have Spirit as your manager or partner than it is to have other people as such. Countless men and women have benefited from turning over difficult problems, as well as minor ones, and decisions and all kinds of choices to Spirit for action.

You will note that the sixth point of the seven under consideration in this book is learning how to turn to God for ideas, then initiating action to bring them forth. Thus God in one aspect will furnish the ideas and in another aspect will carry them out or will produce them. Do not puzzle over this; it was for this purpose we have been taught to regard the one as three. So, if you never have tried asking Spirit to accomplish in your affairs, do so. Find out for yourself if it works. But do not judge by just a few times.

SPIRIT IS THE ONLY MOVER

Rather than a summary of this section, here is a scriptural reference to illustrate the truth that actually we can of ourselves do nothing. We are familiar with "For in Him we live, and move, and have our being." Unfortunately the translators, possibly not understanding

24

the significance, made one important change which they should not have made. This is in the verb *move*. The original Greek, as shown in the Emphatic Diaglott version, says "and are moved" rather than "and move." The phrase actually reads: "For in Him we live, and are moved, and we are." So, whether we believe we move and do the moving or we are moved and only cause to be moved, Spirit is the only mover. But what we believe does make a difference in our being able to do, or to have done, all things. Try it the right way and compare results. You be the judge as to which you wish to accept. That is all that is sought here.

▲

3. THE REAL YOU

ALL ARE SPIRITUAL BEINGS

Man is far more than he seems to be. This applies without exception of sex, color, race, nationality, ancestry or anything else. One who thinks he is favored because of any physical or mental factor cannot achieve his true status until he learns the truth. Woman or man, each is in reality a spiritual being.

In Spirit there is no either male or female, no color of skin, and obviously no nationality or human ancestry. "And call no man your father upon the earth: for One is your Father, which is in heaven." Each is a child of the one Parent. This relationship of God and man as Father and son has been so little understood that it long has been a religious stumbling block. Yet, as the analogy it is, it so simply tells us our relationship with God. Once you grasp this basic truth, you are free from the biggest obstacle to becoming what you really are. Therefore, let us examine this truth.

Father and son may be generalized, with no difficulty in understanding of terms, to parent and child. From there it is a short step to parent and offspring. This is the analogy used by Jesus and others who understand the nature of being. The relationship denoted is a most personal one.

But parent and offspring what? The only thing there really is: Spirit. God is the parent Spirit and all of us are offspring of Spirit. If the term *Spirit* is still too indefinite for you, substitute *Mind* or *Consciousness*. This is the image of God in which we are made, not a physical image in the sense of looking alike.

Then why does not everyone act like a spiritual being? The answer is that, being spiritual, you can act no other way. The difference is in recognition and use. Recognition means knowing what you really are and living at that high level. The fact that you can do or have done anything at all means you possess spiritual attributes and are using spiritual powers. Otherwise you would not be conscious of anything, or at least could not do anything about what you were conscious of, in the world. Use means employing your consciousness at your true level, that of the spiritual plane.

SPIRITUAL INCLUDES ALL REALMS

The spiritual realm is no more separated from us than are the physical and mental realms separated from each other. Do you consider your thinking or mental functioning to be separated completely from the physical world? That would not make sense, would it? We consider the mental or intellectual self to be coexistent with the physical self and world. It is the mental phase that differentiates us from the mineral, plant and animal kingdoms; by which we are able to adapt ourselves to the world, and the world to us. It is also the means by which we enjoy the myriad wonders of the physical world. And there are additional mental pleasures which come, wholly or partially, under the heading of intellectual pursuits. Briefly, the mental realm is far more comprehensive than what we call the physical realm. But the mental includes the physical and is not separate from it.

The spiritual in turn is far more comprehensive than is the mental. But the spiritual includes, and is not separate from, the mental. Therefore, the spiritual is coexistent with or contains the mental and physical, but is also much greater and different. When one has attained to even initial perception of the spiritual realm, he knows there is an awareness above the mental that is greater than mental awareness is above a merely physical state of being. This awareness must include the mental and physical.

In this awareness one sees in some measure the infinite possibilities of spiritual works and pleasures. It would be a truly joyous privilege to speak of some of those which are among the first to be seen and attained; but, even if many would believe, it is only of value to you when you have reached the point where you can see them yourself. "But as it is written, eye has not seen, nor ear heard, neither have entered into the heart of man, the things which God has prepared for them that love Him." They are there. Or to put it more precisely, these glorious wonders God has prepared for us are here, available now. You do not have to go out of this world to obtain

27

them. You no more have to leave your body or this world to attain the spiritual realm than you have to leave your body or this world to attain the mental realm.

HEAVEN IS A STATE OF CONSCIOUSNESS

This is so important, it rates consideration by itself. Do not believe anyone who tells you that you must wait until another world to enter heaven. Heaven is a state of consciousness, the spiritual level of awareness. It is not any particular place or time. It is all places and all times; for God is eternal, and eternity is now. God is Omnipresence, so His kingdom is everywhere. God is forever the same, so there is no future time when He or His heaven is different.

Anyone who tells you that you must leave this body and enter another world before you can achieve this spiritual realm called heaven never has achieved spiritual understanding. Anything which seems to indicate that you cannot achieve spiritual awareness here is either false, as is so much of man's religious dogma, or is commonly misunderstood, as are many of the world's Bibles, including those of the Hebrew and Christian religions. And as for the completely false conception that the Bible cannot be understood fully by man, it is time man stopped believing God to be stupid and spiteful. The key to the interpretation of the Bible now exists for all to see; and for this understanding, the *Metaphysical Bible Dictionary,* by Unity School of Christianity, Unity Village, Missouri, is without equal at this writing.

This is not in the least intended as a tirade against anyone. Instead, it is a stretching forth of a loving hand to those who still believe and those who still teach misconceptions of the spiritual realm. The mental realm is far beyond the comprehension of a being or object that is basically physical. This applies up to, and predominantly including, early man. In like manner but in far greater degree is the spiritual above the intellectual or purely mental. It is truly said that the unillumined intelligence cannot conceive of the spiritual.

But this does not leave man at an impasse. He has but to ask to know God and His spiritual realm, and Spirit, the teacher who knows all things, will reveal these things to him. The question is so often asked, "How can I know there is a God?" It is a wonderful question and one that God so loves to answer. How can you know? The answer is so simple. Just ask God to make Himself known to you. That is all. Sincerely want to know and you will know. But do not try to discover Him by intellectual reasoning, for that is impossible. You must know it, must become aware of it.

So many times do we hear the question, "How did you learn all of this?" There is only one way, and Jesus stated it so perfectly: "Ask and it shall be given you; seek and you shall find; knock and it shall be opened unto you." That is all there is to it: seek or wish this understanding, ask God to provide you with the means of learning about Him, and pay attention to what He shows you. How will you know it is from Him? That too you will learn to know.

To touch a little more on attainment of spiritual awareness here and now, listen to the oft-repeated way Jesus expressed it: "The kingdom of the heavens is at hand," and "Behold, the kingdom of God is within you." Where is "at hand"? Everywhere. What is "within"? Your consciousness. Are you conscious now? Then heaven, paradise, the Garden of Eden, the spiritual realm, spiritual awareness, spiritual consciousness is available now.

Those who do not seek this spiritual consciousness now are in one or more of these categories: not having known it exists at all; not having known it always has existed, and therefore exists now; not having known it is attainable now; believing one is not capable of entering it now, due to past mistakes or other causes; fearful of trying; too disinterested to try or too easily discouraged to continue.

PROVE THESE THINGS YOURSELF

Perhaps some will want to know why they should believe any of this, especially since there have been so many different views expressed by others. We do not ask you to believe what we say. Test it for yourself. Or, what proof can we give? We do not have to give any proof. Prove it yourself and know for yourself. However, countless numbers of men, women and children have been proving it; perhaps even you or your relatives, friends and neighbors, and perhaps entirely unknown to you. Ample proof will be given to those who sincerely ask. Spectacular proofs are occurring constantly and are recognized as such by varying numbers of us.

Yes, actually all of us are proving ourselves to be spiritual offspring of God, our parent Mind, in all we do. The difficulty we have had in recognizing it is that we have been applying our spiritual powers in ignorance, have been applying them in a negative or wrong manner, or have not been applying many of them at all. The fact that you can do anything means you are able to direct Spirit, since Spirit is the only active force. Could anything not a spiritual being consciously direct Spirit? No. Spirit works on and through things which have no spiritual consciousness, but these cannot direct the action of Spirit.

This is the meaning of being made in God's likeness. We are like Him in the nature of our being. Just as the children of man and woman have the same powers as and are able to act like their parents, so is man able to act like God and to use His power, Spirit. Of course, in this world man generally acts in a finite manner, while God is infinite. This is why man is the merging of the infinite and the finite. It is why he partakes of both the infinite and the finite.

Man is God as man when God permits and man so acts. God is man as God when man permits and God so acts. "I Am that I Am." Meditate often on these.

But be not deceived by one who claims to have achieved spiritual awareness and does not act accordingly. How can one not knowing yet the spiritual distinguish between those who have attained and those who only claim it? One who has attained has given us the test to apply: "By their fruits you shall know them." And what is the basis of their fruits, or work? "God is love." Such a person acts only in the best interests of all, with his motive being love. For he or she recognizes the spiritual oneness of all. This oneness is God, the Self of everyone.

MEANING OF "LOVE YOUR NEIGHBOR"

Why does God have no favorites? Why does Jesus say, "Love your neighbor as yourself"? Because the real Self of each and every person is one with God. Therefore, how could God favor any one person? How can you treat the Self of your neighbor, which in general means anyone, as less than Spirit and expect only good? This is what John meant when he said, "If a man says, I love God, and hates his brother, he is a liar." There is only one Spirit and It is at the center of everyone and every created thing. Again, hear and understand Jesus: "You shall love the Lord your God with all your heart, and with all your soul, and with all your mind. This is the first and great commandment. And the second is like unto it, you shall love your neighbor as yourself." *Like unto* means *the same as*.

There has been great bewilderment over this second law. How can you love your neighbor as yourself when you are not supposed to love yourself? The answer lies in the word *self*. There are two selves referred to in such spiritual messages. One is in the image of God; the real Self of each one. The other is the personal self, acting as though separated from God; although separation cannot exist other than in man's lack of recognition or his belief in separation. Therefore, when you love the personal self alone, you are looking away from God. Since the spiritual Self includes the personal self, then you truly love your Self; which is likewise one with God and the spiritual Selves of all others.

EXPRESS YOUR SELF

In this manner do you learn how to know that God is. So do you learn how to know what you really are, as well as what others are, and your relationship to God and to all men and women. From here you can learn how to recognize your oneness with all creation. You learn you have the privilege of using Spirit as power because you are created in the likeness of God, even if you may not have realized it properly and fully. You will learn how to use Spirit as the agent which will create what you properly request.

You will learn how to achieve spiritual awareness, followed by spiritual growth. You will learn how to manifest the glory God glorified you with from the beginning, even before this particular world or system of things began physical manifestation. You will learn how to enjoy the real life prepared for you in heaven, eternally. Are these not sufficient how-to's to warrant such a title for a book as *How To Do All Things*? It does not mean anyone else can do this for you; that is not possible. You must learn how to do, and then do, them yourself.

How can you learn to do them yourself? By yourself you cannot. But by your Self you can learn to do, and then do by having done, all things. For your Self is ever nigh unto you, even "closer than breathing" is your real Self, always awaiting your recognition and desire for at-onement. We recognize and salute your Self, knowing you thereby come to do the same for yourself and all others. Even so, now know as you are known. So be it.

▲

4. DIVINE POWER IS YOURS ACCORDING TO YOUR DEGREE OF SPIRITUAL EXPRESSING

COMMAND PERFORMANCE

"Concerning the work of my hands, command me." Command performance: you command, Spirit performs.

Yes, all your life Spirit has been performing as you have commanded. You already have seen how this is so. Even though you knew it not, you spoke the words aloud or silently that activated intelligent and obedient power to accomplish for you.

Acting in physical awareness you issued orders which resulted in the action of Spirit in physical ways. You wished to move and you were moved. You wished to perform various acts of work or play and they were performed through you. Spirit serves you most well indeed in the physical world. Much also is performed for you that you need not ask for specifically, such as automatic body functions and many actions in nature. We also must remember that "God said" and the moving force has created and has maintained all physical manifestations.

Acting in mental or intellectual awareness you, representing mankind, have issued orders which resulted in Spirit bringing you ideas and then producing both physical and intellectual creations for you as you developed and applied these ideas. You have not sought always the advice of God when ideas are needed, but fortunately you have received many anyhow. So many times, though, when you wondered how to protect yourself from the weather, how to provide for your basic needs of food and clothing, how to make work easier, how to make life more pleasurable, and how to accomplish countless other objectives, Spirit has worked for you in the intellectual realm. Nor has It performed only when you first recognized It and then gave thanks.

Acting in supposed spiritual awareness, man of Earth has not issued relatively many requests which have resulted in action at the spiritual level. Why is this so? Has not man for thousands of years thought he had enough spiritual awareness to ask God for many things? Yet, comparatively few such prayers have been answered in the requested manner. Why? Sometimes it has been due to asking for the wrong thing or not recognizing the answer when it or a better one came. But this is not the major cause of unanswered requests on the spiritual level to what are commonly called prayers. "You ask, and receive not, because you ask amiss." This is a broad topic, one which is more properly the subject of the next section.

"Hitherto have you asked nothing in my name." To initiate action in the spiritual realm you must ask in your spiritual awareness. Jesus was speaking of this spiritual awareness when making that statement. He spoke in the Christ consciousness, which is the awareness of one who has attained to the inherent spiritual perfection. Is not your name really the identification of your consciousness? The ultimate meaning of this advice by Jesus is that most have not asked yet for anything in the spiritual consciousness. Can you achieve and speak in this awareness? "The things I do, ye shall do."

Then why is it Spirit does many things for us without our asking? Why, when we are not operating in spiritual awareness, does Spirit sometimes answer our requests and sometimes not? Would Spirit always answer our requests once we have achieved the second birth, the spiritual awakening? Does Spirit favor any of us or does It act in an impersonal manner? These are important questions, but the answers have been known by many others, and now by you.

Spirit as working force does much for us without our asking or even knowing, because God so has established such work. These workings prescribed by God include the creation, maintenance and functioning of the body. They also include what is called nature. All this has been ordained and has been established by divine decree. In some of these works man has interfered, bringing about disharmony. In some works he cannot interfere, due to lack of understanding or inability to do so.

There are many occasions when Spirit does perform according to your requests even though you have not been acting with spiritual understanding. These include those things already mentioned, such as requests for body movement and works performed through machinery and such forces as electricity and chemistry. Again, these are possible because God so has established His universal law that what we refer to as individual laws prevail. These laws are the same on each level of consciousness, so our initiating action on any level will cause Spirit to act according to these laws. In this manner, because God has established these ways in which His power acts according to thought, we do exercise a certain amount of initiative control over the activation of power. This is so even when we have not achieved or are not acting in spiritual awareness. This is also the manner in which the less evolved forms of what is mistakenly called life are able to cause action.

IMPROPER REQUESTING

As for not answering our requests, there may be several reasons why this either is or appears to be so. You may be having done what you really asked be done, thinking you were asking for something else. Or you may be obstructing the carrying out of your request because of your changing or canceling it, also without your knowledge of doing so. At other times you may be asking for something that cannot be accomplished because it is contrary to natural law. Or you may not have fulfilled certain qualifications which are necessary before your request can be enacted. Also, your requests may not be decisive or selective enough. All these are covered by "You ask, and receive not, because you ask amiss." However, as this is a topic that warrants considerable attention, it is, as previously stated, discussed in the next section, devoted to the fifth point.

Nor could Spirit possibly play favorites. "God is no respecter of persons." Of course, this could not mean God has no respect or concern for individual persons, but it does mean His divine law is impersonal. Electricity is an impersonal force, yet it is a form of divine power. It is extremely important that you know this: God never punishes anyone. This is impossible, as God is love. It is man's attempts to go contrary to impersonal law that result in the consequences called punishment. Does electricity consciously punish one who uses it contrary to its laws or is this an impersonal case of cause and effect? To repeat this truth for emphasis: God does not punish anyone. What seem to be punishments are the effects caused by violating impersonal divine law. Such mistakes, known or unknown, are referred to in religion as sins.

DEGREES OF SPIRITUAL UNDERSTANDING

The remaining question of those advanced several paragraphs ago is whether Spirit always would enact your request once you had experienced spiritual awareness. The answer to this is the fourth of the seven points or studies: the degree of responsiveness of Spirit to your requests for action depends on the degree to which you live up to your inherent spiritual nature. Therefore, let us delve into this matter of degrees of spiritual living.

Starting with no degree of spiritual awareness, we have seen that we can rely on having Spirit act for us only within the confines of certain divine laws. This is worth your most earnest attention because it is why man seems bound by physical laws. He is so bound only because he has not seen how to invoke Spirit action which can and would take him outside those bonds. This does not mean miracles, for since divine laws cannot be broken there are no miracles possible. Such actions are really due to man's recognition of his inherent ability to speak for himself rather than be spoken for by laws. Such laws are necessary until you are able to function beyond their automatic assistance.

Jesus or anyone else cannot perform miracles. Man has been denied his own ability to do these works not by those who can have them done but because of misunderstanding. Nor do the scriptural accounts of these acts by Jesus mean to call them miracles, as the word commonly is interpreted today. *Signs* or *works* better expresses the meaning. These works, and infinite others, can be done by anyone who attains the necessary spiritual understanding. Many of these, and countless others, are being performed continuously by many people. "The works I do, ye shall do." Note the verb Jesus used: *shall,* not *can*. He used *shall* for the reason that eventually everyone will attain spiritual perfection. Then all shall do these, and other, works.

We previously discussed supposed spiritual awareness which, since it is not genuine, cannot pass as real in the spiritual realm. The actual nature of the awareness is what determines it, not man's definition or claim. So, this man-made spirituality counts for naught.

Assuming one has had a spiritual awakening, does it follow that he or she thereafter always will enjoy the full use of divine powers? No, not automatically. Some have experienced this awakening without knowing what it was. It may have existed for them only for a matter of what man calls minutes and not have been achieved again. While such persons may retain some of the effects of that experience for years and it may completely change their lives, they only experienced it; they did not learn how to use the powers available in that realm. Therefore, while knowing the spiritual realm does exist, they are not able to remain and thus to function in that consciousness.

At but a little higher level is one who has attained some degree of spiritual understanding but does not make much effort to use what he has learned, let alone gain more. Haphazard and partial use can bring such a one more difficulty than one who knows nothing of these things. And woe unto the one who tries to use spiritual power in adverse ways! Since Spirit cannot act against Itself and so disrupt divine order and harmony, such a person would reap consequences of grave nature.

Finally, there is the one who knows something of spiritual things but does not choose always to act according to these principles. Since he has achieved a greater measure of use of power, any misdirection can bring him inharmony. Such a person knows better, so must act better or lose somewhere. "He that doeth, much will be done through him; but he that does not, will have taken from him all that can be done with and through him."

SPIRITUAL GROWTH NECESSARY

Why is it that once one has attained to spiritual awareness, and thus has been born again, he does not achieve fully and permanently? Because it is just as being born physically: you then must grow. One experiencing physical birth is not automatically fully developed physically and mentally. He must grow and learn to use his physical and mental powers. Spiritual rebirth is similar. You must learn and use what you learn in order to develop spiritual awareness. It is important also to know that you cannot expect to continue to acquire spiritual understanding until you reach a certain level before you put it to use. It is infinite. You must begin to use it as you learn it or your growth stops, and even retrogresses. "Faith without works is dead."

In order to progress spiritually, one must live up to his spiritual nature. But what is this spiritual nature? There are many religious and other beliefs that try to convince man of some particular answer, or even of no answer or no spiritual nature at all. Surely all cannot be right. Then how is man to know what constitutes spiritual awareness? How can one attain it when there are so many contradictory claims? Some say man cannot know or achieve spiritual awareness in this Earthly existence. This is not true; man can know and achieve here, and countless numbers of women and men have done so.

Much valuable information has been given to us by those who do know man's spiritual nature; in the form of talks, writings, actions and deeds. All such illumined ones teach the same truth, which can be summed up briefly in but a few words. You are created a spiritual being. Therefore, once you know this you need not search anywhere for this truth; it is within you and is part of you. If you will accept the reality that God created you, and that God creates only perfection, you need only sincerely ask that you manifest on Earth the perfection you already have in heaven. Heaven is the realm of spiritual perfection; earth is the manifestation of that perfection.

SEEK SPIRITUAL PERFECTION

It is a divine law that what you think of earnestly and sincerely will tend to come to pass for you. If you will hold constantly before you the manifesting of your spiritual perfection, you will be taught how to achieve it. Your teacher will be the only instructor who knows all things, including you. Yes, that teacher is God, and His school is within your own consciousness.

At first you will not be able always to know what you should do. That is because you have not learned fully yet the spiritual language and so are not aware of the instruction. But do not despair, for you will be taught, by God within your own consciousness, the true language and how to understand His teachings. Also, in the beginning you will make mistakes. Again, do not let this overly disturb you, for as long as you really wish to achieve the perfection which was established for you from the beginning, those mistakes will not be serious.

Let your guide be divine love. In your thoughts and actions toward others, consider not what an imperfectly manifesting man might think and do but rather what God thinks and does. The thoughts of God cannot be less than loving; neither should yours be. Divine love sees all creation as perfect. If you see it less than perfect, you are not seeing perfectly. Double-talk? Not at all; meditate on that thought until its meaning comes to you.

But what if another is acting in a manner that obviously seems less than perfect? "What is that to you? Follow me." This is the instruction of the spiritual Self within. You can never achieve perfection if you think in terms of less than perfection. Is not acceptance of imperfection in itself proof that one has not achieved perfection? "You are of purer eyes than to behold evil."

Perhaps it puzzles you to hear that all is perfection, and therefore the spiritually aware see only perfection, when the world seems to reveal much imperfection. The answer is really simple: "Judge not according to appearance, but judge righteous judgment." Note the words *seem* in the first sentence of this paragraph and *appearance* in the second. Both mean the same in this connection. What appears to man as imperfection only seems so to him.

As you progress in your spiritual education, you will learn to see the perfection or reality behind all things and actions. When you have reached this level, you will find that the seeming imperfections in the world cannot affect you, either because they do not exist in reality or because they are not the imperfections which others believe. Jesus said, "If therefore your eye be single, your whole body shall be full of light." Or in modern language, when you see only perfection your whole life is filled with only truth. Then it will come to pass for you that you do not even think of perfection; for perfection brings to thought its contrast of imperfection. In reality, as God made and sees them, all things only are, and this means even beyond definition as perfect.

LIVE UP TO YOUR SPIRITUAL NATURE

Does this mean one even cannot begin spiritual progress, since at first he does not live up to his spiritual nature? One does not see any reason to attempt to gain that which is hopeless. Yet this is exactly what much religious dogma has held before man. How? By telling him, through literal rather than spiritual interpretation of his Bibles, that he is an evil creation and that he cannot attain perfection and heaven on Earth. This is one of the greatest sins or errors ever committed against man. Truly the blind have led the blind and both have fallen into the ditch of human limitations. Turn now from these self-proclaiming spiritually ignorant ones to one who has achieved spiritual awareness. "Is it not written in your law, I said, you are gods?"

Yes, one can begin spiritual progress, which when faithfully followed must inevitably lead to perfection, right now. Actually, there is no other time for starting than now. For whenever one does begin, and all must, it is now for him at such time of starting. "Now is the accepted time." Not at some distant place and time, for whatever that place and time you then will say, "It is here and now that I begin." Eternity is always now. Since you are created a perfect spiritual being, you exist eternally in the now. You are immortal, so get to your spiritual life right now and cease with human limitations.

Living up to the spiritual nature, as used here, means perceiving that spiritual nature and doing one's best to live up to it at the level of awareness where one is. This is all that is ever asked of you: that you think and act as best you know how while seeking to know the best there is, God; "For in Him we live, and are moved, and we are." As you do this, you cannot help but experience spiritual rebirth and growth.

TESTS OF TEACHINGS

To assist us in obtaining this spiritual awareness and growth, God has given many guides. All of His creations serve in some way to instruct. This includes man. For although our highest teacher is within our own consciousness, He lovingly has revealed the way by means of His works through man, His highest expression on this Earth. But beware of those men and women who, knowingly or unknowingly, speak from the personal self rather than as the spiritual Self. Such delay not only their own spiritual awakening but also that of those who heed them.

How can one distinguish between those who lead astray and those who light the way? This is no easy task, and no attempt shall be made here to enter the subject deeply. But there are some general tests which will help one to save time, effort and experiences. This does not mean all the teachings of a group or individual are valueless if these general tests are not met. However, it does signify one thereafter should proceed cautiously rather than accept blindly and completely all that is taught by that source.

GOD DOES NOT PUNISH

God is love. Therefore, do not accept any teaching that He is ever angry with or punishes man. Those who believe this to be true have not perceived divine love yet, although eventually they will. Man long has sought to remake God according to man's image, or how man imagines God. Fortunately this is not reality. It has been man whose limited concept of love has recognized imperfection and who has decreed punishment for those whom he did not love, and often even for those he did. Divine love is truly what makes the world, and all creation, go around or exist. God cannot hate and cannot punish man, for He knows naught of such things.

It is not that God forgives, either, for one only forgives what he thinks to have been an imperfect or improper act against him or another. Rather than forgiving, God understands. Understanding means knowing one was acting in such manner only because he really did not know better, even though it seemed he did. For if he really knew better he would not have acted that way. Furthermore, forgiveness implies an act against someone; man cannot harm God.

If God does not punish man, why does it seem so? It is because man punishes himself by acting contrary to divine laws. These are impersonal and in no manner due to judgments by God. His judgment of you is that you are His perfect offspring. What is your judgment of Him, and of yourself? Ignorance of divine laws is no excuse. But man has sought to place the blame for disharmony in his life everywhere but where it belongs. He blames God, or an allegorical devil, or someone else, or chance, or superstitious beliefs and many other things, when usually it is he who is to blame.

If God is not wrathful and vengeful, why do the Bibles say so? They do not, to those who are able to read them spiritually, as is intended. The materially minded see the Hebrew Testament recounting brutal tales of God causing many to be destroyed; the spiritually illumined see those same stories as instructions for overcoming one's own error thoughts. The uninformed see suffering and death throughout the entire Christian Bible; the informed see overcoming and life in the same passages. One sees God punishing those who have sinned against His laws; the other sees man punishing himself due to a mistaken act contrary to divine law. God is divine love, and this love does not contain the error concepts of hate and punishment that human love does.

OTHER TESTS FOR VALIDITY

A second test is in the nature and location of heaven and of hell. Neither are some place or of some future destination. Both refer only to states of consciousness wherein one may be at any time. This applies to the way one experiences life, be it on this Earth in this life or in some other world at some other time. Anyone who really reads the words of Christ Jesus, for example, can plainly see this. Not so easily seen are the Hebrew and Christian references to hell, which actually refer either to the grave or to Gehenna, a dump where refuse was burned, which references are known by earnest Bible students. Thus heaven and hell are not places where a judging God sends man once he completes his Earthly existence. God already has placed man in heaven; He made no hell. Man either accepts and enjoys God's heaven or makes his own version of heaven or hell.

Of a similar nature to this last test is the one concerning man's ability to achieve perfection. Since this already has been discussed, it only will be added that man should begin his spiritual development where he finds himself now. If one continually puts off such a beginning until a future life, he will be doing so eternally. This does not mean forever, for *eternally* as used in the Bibles often means to the end of an age or the end of a way of thinking. Where can you start? Where you are now. When can you start? You are eternal, so would it not be wise to begin now, thus eliminating undesirable experiences and achieving your destined happiness that much sooner?

Another test is the naming of the means of instruction. Let man stop selling his birthright of freedom of will to any group or individual claiming to be the only way of instruction. Let him no longer be misled by those who tell him they are the only contacts between God and man. God created man as His means of expressing to enjoy His other creations and to be cocreators. For that purpose He is one with the true Self of each person, and cannot be told by man that He cannot express so directly. Man has only to turn to God within his own thinking to commune with Him. God and man are one. God, who dwells within man, does not need to turn to any dogma, symbolization or man-made organization to express as man. So long as one thinks so, just so long does he deny himself his true expression of God.

Those who understand this may assist you to learn, but they always tell you they seek only to guide you until you can recognize and hear the prime teacher, Spirit, which instructs you in all understanding, from within your own consciousness. Follow not those who claim they are the only real teachers, but rather listen to those who say the teacher is within you and is always directly accessible to you. Nor let them tell you that Jesus claimed to be the way; for they do not perceive that it was the Christ or real Self who spoke and not Jesus the man, who never sought worshippers.

As stated earlier, there are many tests which can be applied to determine somewhat the validity of the many claims to spiritual understanding. But for now suffice it to say that those who have achieved spiritual rebirth will tell you: you are created perfectly, in the image and likeness of God; God dwells within you; you need no intercessor to commune with God, although it will hasten your progress; you are no worse and no better than anyone else, for all are created equal; God never punishes, but loves you and is eager to teach you how to avoid mistakes; you can achieve spiritual perfection here on Earth; and also, all of God's creations are perfect, even though they may not appear or not act so. Again, remember this is not a tirade against any group or individual, for there is at least some value to most religious teachings. But just as children put aside many fantasies as they grow to manhood, so must man discard fantasies and fallacies as he passes from the mortal to the spiritual.

In this brief manner have you been acquainted with sufficient knowledge of your true, the spiritual, nature to enable you to begin acting therein. But remember the earlier statement that it is not enough just to experience the birth of spiritual awareness in order to achieve full awareness. You must grow spiritually, even as you must grow physically and mentally. This does not mean the growth necessarily will be fast, effortless and painless. That is up to you.

Consequently, the fourth study, the degree of responsiveness of Spirit to your requests for action, depends on the degree to which you live up to your inherent spiritual nature. That inherent nature is perfect, actually even beyond classification as perfect, so do not expect always to act perfectly until you have reached perfection. But do not let this become a limitation in your envisioning the person you seek to become. Do not say you are not acting perfectly now, but rather that you are rapidly manifesting the perfection which already is yours. In the first instance you would be seeing imperfection; in the second you would be seeing the perfection, even though sometimes you did not understand situations sufficiently to avoid mistakes. But a mistake is not permanent; perfection is.

Therefore, even though you may make mistakes in your early attempts to learn how to direct the moving force, do not let that prevent your growth. Rather than blame God or someone else, try to discover the lesson taught by the mistake and keep learning to do better. The more completely you discover your Self and the more you act as your Self, the more you accomplish in your role of co-creation, co-operation and co-enjoyment with God.

44

It would be well also, in closing this fourth study, to remember it is not sufficient, in our proper requesting of Spirit to act for us, merely to have spiritual awareness. We also must live up to it as best we know how. Creative Force does not perform for us at higher levels just because we know It can. It performs only for those who are able to direct It according to divine law. This is because It acts as we think. When we think less than spiritually, It knows we really are aware we are not asking in a spiritual manner, and thus really do not wish to have work done at that level.

This is important and bears study until you fully understand. It is the reason God need not judge man, for he judges himself by the way in which he thinks and acts. He knows how he thinks; and since God and he are one, so also does God at all times know what he thinks. God and man exist in and think with the only Mind there is: Divine Mind. Think divine thoughts and have Spirit do divine things for you.

▲

5. LEARNING TO USE DIVINE POWER

UNDERSTAND YOUR SELF

By now you consciously have become aware of your true nature. You have learned you are not merely a physical body with a brain which enables you to think. You now know, even though you may not as yet have become convinced consciously, that you are in reality a spiritual being. This spiritual you includes the physical and mental you with which you are familiar. Rather than your brain being the reason you can think, it is actually the medium through which your thoughts are transformed into action in your mental and physical worlds.

We greet spiritual you and see you rapidly unfolding your perfect Self. You were greeted thus with divine love as you began to read this book, but it was done in a spiritual manner which you did not recognize unless you already had achieved a certain degree of spiritual awareness. That greeting was one of the influencing factors which brought you this far.

This may not mean you have done much more than begin to recognize yourself. To repeat: one does not achieve spiritual adulthood in one easy step. There is much to unlearn before and while you learn what you are destined to know. Therefore, you may have much work ahead. You will find this to be the most exciting and fascinating endeavor possible, the discovery and understanding of your Self. You never will cease this spiritual unfolding, for it is eternal. Truly has it been said that "Eye has not seen, nor ear heard, neither have entered into the heart of man, the things which God has prepared for them that love Him."

So far you have been told numerous times: as you decree, Spirit does that which you have asked. But you have had no explanation of what is meant by decreeing; proper or improper, conscious and unconscious. This is because it is first necessary that you not only know who and what you really are but that you also begin to act it.

46

You always have had this knowledge within, but since you must learn to act as a conscious center of free will, it is necessary that it come to your conscious attention.

Your conscious will is given divine precedence over your entire mortal being; otherwise you would not be a divine expression, in the image and likeness of God. This is why you are permitted to do essentially as you wish, even though the Self within you knows what will happen when you either initiate a certain action or do not prevent it. You must learn to do or to have done through your conscious willing. In this manner does the infinite express finitely; the great impersonal as individual personality. This mystery may be too deep for many as yet, but eventually all will know as they are known.

Just one more aid before discussing the subject of proper decreeing, or speaking the word. This is not only invaluable at the beginning of your spiritual journey but is something which must be done sooner or later anyway. Doing it at the start both will speed your unfoldment and will make it far easier. It is indeed well that you begin your study of proper decreeing here and that you give this point repeated attention.

You just read that although your inner Self knows all things, including what you should do and what will result if you do otherwise, for the most part it will not interfere with the decisions of your conscious will. This is almost invariably true, even though it might mean dire consequences for you, including the transition man mistakenly calls death. However, this does not mean your Self did not advise you. It may be that you did not recognize the advice or that you ignored it, not knowing the source. For there is always one with you as your guide. Call this one what you will: superconsciousness, guardian angel, Father, Self, Christ, Jehovah, Atman or others; but call.

Yes, call. Call in the beginning and call often, until you fully understand you need not call your Self because you are that Self. If this does not seem to make sense, simply pass it by for now. The time will come when you will understand. But now, call in the following manner.

Since in the beginning of our spiritual awakening we do not know consciously how to do all things properly, we will expect to make mistakes. Also, and in one way far more important, we do not know all the mistakes we already have made or the mistakes of others which we have accepted as right. Since our already accepted thinking is what influences action up to this new birth, we must make certain our basic thinking is right.

Our fundamental physical and mental nature is influenced not only through what we have gained from our own prior experiences and learning but also by what has been experienced and has been believed by our families, friends, associates, groups, fellow citizens and mankind for many thousands of years. This in general is called race thought. Obviously we cannot hope to trace back every thought we ever have accepted, let alone those of others which unknowingly have influenced us, to see if we should accept or reject them.

There are many things you have stored in your memory storehouse that must be brought to your conscious attention for you once more to judge. But know in advance the nature of this calling to your attention, so you will not fear. You are the only one who really ever can judge you. God does not judge you anew. He judged you in the beginning when He pronounced you perfect. No other one is permitted to judge you unless you so permit and accept that judgment.

So, if the thoughts you have held, which include the things you have done or have had done by your thinking, are rerun through your consciousness, know they have not been brought forth to judge and to condemn you but are up for you to judge and to condemn or to accept them. This is a vitally important point to remember. Many have fallen back here, believing they are unworthy, condemned, sacrilegious, lost or otherwise unable to express perfection.

So face up to these thoughts, know that you and not they are judge of you, and pass judgment on these things you have thought and have done. Some you may be able to dismiss at once, some may require persistent attention and action, some may require your righting a wrong, and some may be put aside until you are better able to pass judgment, to decree properly. But do not neglect them or permit them to have any power over you. Dispose of them rather than let them continue in the same way.

Fortunately, however, it is not necessary that we trace back and pass judgment on every thought that still in some manner influences our thinking. Man has tried to do so and thereby has perpetuated many of his bonds and much unnecessary grief and hardship. Man made a grave error in studying his past in terms of hatred and cruelty to his fellowman. He could not see that he continued to bring forth that upon which his attention was focused from early childhood. The proper study of the past is the bringing forth of the spiritual nature of man, for by focusing our attention on the perfect, we tend to hasten its inevitable manifestation.

But since your world must be set right first within your own consciousness, you must make certain there are no error thoughts still influencing your thinking. You cannot achieve complete spiritual perfection so long as you retain any error ideas, even if you consciously are not aware they still exist in your memory; or subconsciously, if you prefer the term.

ELIMINATING ERROR THOUGHTS

It is hoped by now you are asking how to eliminate them if you are not aware of them. For unless you also want to have them eliminated, you are not serious enough about your spiritual education. However, by now you are serious. The answer to this apparent dilemma may already have come to those of you who have not put it into practice. Whether it has or not, learn of it now. What are we speaking of throughout this book? How to do all things. How? Ask Spirit to do it.

Yes, this too ask Spirit to do and it will be done. Earlier in this fifth study it was pointed out that your real Self knows all necessary things. But it also was stated that seldom will your Self interfere with your right of conscious free will. Let us talk for a while in terms of superconscious, conscious and subconscious phases of your total being. We will call the superconscious your Self, the conscious your outer awareness or will, and the subconscious your administrator that relays your decrees to Creative Energy for enactment.

The superconscious knows all necessary things and is able to supply you with whatever information your conscious self wishes. Of course, you must learn how to recognize this information as it is given. This is the purpose of the sixth study, where you will learn that the answer is available even before you ask, for your Self knows what you want. "Before they call, I will answer; and while they are yet speaking, I will hear." But your conscious self must make the decision.

Your subconscious then unquestioningly accepts that decision, acting upon it or storing it for use in future actions. Since these stored thoughts of yours, as well as those you inherit from mankind and those that filter in daily from other sources, will influence most of your initiating of action even though you are not aware of it each time, you must see to it that you have only true thoughts so stored. Then the moving force will receive only proper and clear requests through your administrative subconscious.

HIGH SELF AS GUIDE AND CHECK

Continuing this matter of asking Spirit to eliminate error thoughts, your subconscious accepts the decisions made by your conscious self, when both are operating properly. But you can set up a guide and a check on what you wish to be recorded by your subconscious. This is of great importance, as it is the way in which you not only cause to be eliminated all error thoughts you do not, and often cannot, recall in your memory but in which you can prevent future mistaken thoughts, by you or others, from being recorded.

This guide and check is your superconscious, your Self. To receive this perfect help, all you need do, in effect, is tell your subconscious that your superconscious henceforth is to be the final judge as to what is recorded, even to the point of changing your conscious decisions, any and all of them. Then make it known that your superconscious has your conscious request and permission to eliminate all error thoughts now stored in memory. In essence you are asking your Self to help your self guide you. Since you consciously have asked Spirit, through your real Self, to aid in making decisions, your divine right of free will is not violated.

The New Testament refers to this elimination of error thoughts by Spirit as cleansing by fire. In the mythology of Hercules' twelve tasks, this cleansing is portrayed by his diverting the stream to clean the stables—the waste in the stables representing error thoughts in the memory storehouse—thus having nature do for him what he alone could not have done. There are many other accounts of this cleansing by Spirit throughout religion and literature, so it is not original in this book. However, if this is the first time you have learned of it, do not be dismayed that you did not know it before; put it to use now, for now is the only time you really have. When the past was here, it was now; when the future is here, it will be now.

The wording of your request, and thereby permission, for your Self to eliminate stored error thoughts and to act as final guide and check on all your thoughts henceforth is not in itself sufficient. What are important are the feeling and the sincerity behind your request. Your feeling is the important thing underlying all of your decrees; what you really believe and how you believe it, not merely the thoughts or words in themselves. Remember well this point, for it is a key to your effective invoking of spiritual action.

A word of further explanation and caution in this connection. Do not think Spirit or your Self hereby will make all decisions for you. There are many you must make for yourself. When there are some your Self would effect, you will become aware of them consciously, one way or another. This may be through intuitive flashes, through another person, through an event or other media, or even by going against your conscious will. But remember you really are that Self and are on the way to conscious oneness with the spiritual being you were created. As for the necessity of making conscious decisions, if you do not learn to do it for yourself, your Self will see to it that you do, by letting your self make all decisions.

To summarize this first important step in learning how to decree properly, as well as preventing improper decrees by you and others from affecting you: ask Spirit to eliminate all error thoughts from your thinking. Know that God is doing this, and give thanks to Him that it is being done. Believe it is being done. In this paragraph you have the key steps to having things done for you by Spirit: (1) recognizing God as the source of all that is, and therefore also of all true

51

knowledge and power to create; (2) asking God for His assistance; (3) believing that He is even now granting your request; and (4) giving thanks to Him for already having started the manifestation of your request.

So far you have learned it is the divine plan that you, a spiritual being, are to cause things to be created and to be enacted by your decrees, while Spirit plays the role of creative and enacting agent. Even though you did not at first know this, it was always so. You also know that God will provide the ideas and information, as well as carry out what you desire. Eventually you will come to see, if you do not know already, that this is not the unnecessary action between God as knower, man as thinker and God as doer that it seems, but that in its highest operation it is really three phases of one knower-thinker-doer. If this is not clear as yet or if you tend to be apprehensive about it, do not try to force your understanding. It will come to you in due time, for the seed always has existed within you. This is but one of many stirrings toward flowering of that seed.

ACT IN YOUR SPIRITUAL CAPACITY

The work now at hand is the method of proper decreeing. It is neither possible nor desirable to go into extensive detail on this subject here. The theme of this book is to show you how to obtain what you want and not how to get it all at once, for that is impossible. Therefore, as you learn some of these basics about proper decreeing, you will be able to apply them to ask for additional information, which Spirit will bring to your attention in many ways. Do not in this or other matters attempt to tell Spirit how it must be done, for Spirit knows all things and you do not.

However, both with the information on decreeing you receive here and with other information you receive elsewhere and here, test and prove by continual application. You are not asked to accept something that has not been proved and that you cannot prove also. But do not give up if you are not successful the first few times, for it often takes much work to unlearn improper information and then to learn what is proper. Man has much misinformation to unlearn before he can learn more truth.

You now know that all decreeing should be done with the knowledge that you are spiritual. This applies to everything in your life; for your life is spiritual life which includes, and is not separate from, your mental and physical life. You must learn there is no real separation; all is spiritual. As you think more and more in this way, you quickly see and act only spiritually. Then you are back in your true home, the spiritual realm, from which you were never really absent; you just thought so.

This knowing everything as spiritual is most important, as it establishes your right to decree and to have done ever greater works. Earlier in this fifth study it was mentioned that a vitally important part of speaking the word is the feeling behind the decree; or request, prayer, affirmation, command, visualization, realization, or whatever you use. A large part of this background feeling is knowing the authority which you have been given, and now have begun to accept, to speak the word that causes Spirit to act for you.

In the beginning, when asking for proper things, you should preface your decree with the statement that you now are speaking in your spiritual capacity and therefore you know it will be done for you as you ask. Gradually you will find it less and less necessary to repeat this; your awareness becomes ever more saturated with this deep conviction, and it becomes firmly established that you consciously act in your spiritual capacity. Only as you increase this acting according to your spiritual nature will you be given higher understanding. In this manner you consciously train yourself in spiritual growth until you have manifested your real Self.

As this occurs you do not lose your personal identity but greatly enlarge and enhance it, just as your physical and mental growth made you far more an individual personality. Therefore, do not believe that spiritual growth eventually leads to less pleasure or to absorption into Divine Mind. In reality you eternally experience ever-increasing pleasure and all-around living beyond man's present conception. Rather than losing your identity within Divine Mind, you actually gain more expression of Divine Mind within you. It is truly a glorious adventure.

Much of this fifth study so far may have seemed to diverge from the topic of proper decreeing. But it is all a necessary part of establishing your proper identity and thus your right to initiate action by Spirit. You may compare it to the training given a prince so when he assumes kingship he is convinced completely of his right to issue decrees. Then his requests are issued easily and simply, with no further need to convince himself, his government or his people that he is king and must be obeyed.

Your kingdom far surpasses an Earthly kingdom, and it already has been prepared for you. All you need do is learn to assume your authority. The government of your kingdom is divine law. The people of your kingdom are your own thoughts. This is the analogy the Hebrew, Christian and other Bibles use: kings represent the personal conscious self, and people represent the thoughts of that self. All hail the newborn king!

Now briefly into the essentials of issuing a proper decree. Briefly because it is well for you to meditate upon them while asking Spirit for more information about them, and because you should explore others of the many excellent works on the subject. Where and what are these other works? Do not concern yourself about that for now. Just ask Spirit to be your guide in finding them. Make certain, though, that you heed this guiding.

Actually, all of these essentials for proper visualization can be summed up by saying you always should act according to your inherent spiritual nature. Or more concisely, that God is all. "I Am God, and there is none else." But since at first man does not remember now what this means, he must learn through various ways and experiences. It will prove interesting to you, as you study the points discussed in this section, to see that each one does say the same thing: act in your spiritual nature.

ALWAYS THINK POSITIVELY

You must learn always to think properly and positively. The New Testament phrases it, "Pray without ceasing"; always think positively. When you think both properly and improperly, or positively and negatively, about one thing, you obviously cannot issue a coherent or decisive decree. You cannot ask for one thing to happen and yet expect it not to happen. Spirit cannot provide you with what you want and what you do not want at the same time.

For example, you cannot ask Spirit to cause a certain dis-ease to be eliminated and at the same time believe it will not be eliminated. You could apply well the basic law that an action continues until another action causes it to change. Or, a certain condition may continue to exist until you cause it to change by proper decree. You may have some difficulty at first in thinking properly and positively, but as you persist you will find it to be the natural thing to do.

Of course, you cannot think positively when you are harboring negative thoughts about yourself or others. The best way to overcome that is by constantly seeing both others and yourself as spiritual beings. Do not allow yourself to dwell on any unpleasant subject such as grief, fear or any problem in a negative manner. Instead, know that your Self is aware of the problem and the solution, and ask for help. Then dwell briefly on how you will feel when the problem has been eliminated, and then forget it, thus clearing your thinking for other matters of proper living.

In everything allow only positive and proper thoughts to remain in your consciousness. Sometimes it may be sufficient just to eliminate conscious negative thoughts. At other times it is necessary to do more: you must replace negative thoughts in your memory storehouse with positive ones. This is why it is sometimes difficult at first to have positive conscious thoughts materialize in pleasant events; the negative thoughts in your mental storehouse are too firmly entrenched and must be cleared out. You can and will do it.

In order to decree positively, you cannot think negatively. You cannot ask for and receive happiness by constantly saying, "I am unhappy." Nor can you ask for and receive health, prosperity, understanding, friends and love by saying, "I am sick, poor, ignorant, friendless and unloved." In reality you get what you really ask for, directly or by expectation.

Does this sound strange? But it is true, by the very nature of your being. Since you always have been a spiritual being, even though you knew it not for a while, many of your decrees were manifested by impersonal creating power. Thus is one the cause of much of his own misfortune; because negative as well as positive decrees, up to certain levels, are not analyzed by the moving force.

This is why it is so important for one to learn to decree, within the realm of possibility, what he wants manifested. In many things this automatically eliminates what he does not want manifested. For example, when you realize and so decree that there is nothing which can frighten you, automatically you prevent any fears from finding you. Similarly, when you decree that you can manifest only perfect health, eventually no illness can beset you. This degree of realization takes conscious effort to achieve, but many have achieved it or you would not read about it here. Also, thereafter you cannot act deliberately contrary to what you know you should, and still expect no consequences. You must live up to your spiritual nature.

RELEASE ACTION TO SPIRIT

Another basic point is the extent of your decree. You decide what you want and establish it by decree. It is not within the function of your decree that you try to bring it to pass through willpower. Your decree is not the force that manifests itself; Spirit is that force. All you do is hold the request in your conscious thought sufficiently long to convince yourself it will be acted upon by Spirit. At first this may require considerable convincing, but it becomes easier; until you reach the stage where you no longer need any convincing, for the very act of decreeing automatically assumes the knowledge that your decrees are effective.

As soon as you have convinced yourself it will be acted upon— or, during your initial trials, that you sincerely want to expect it to work—release the request to Spirit for action. Do not attempt to force it to completion or to dictate how it should be done, for by so doing you have not released it to intelligent power. Again, command performance: you command, Spirit performs. Of course, by now you are not upset over the use of the words *command* and *decree,* for you know they are not used in a manner denoting your supremacy or Spirit's inferiority.

In considering this releasing of your decree to Spirit for action, do not take back the power you gave by in any way meddling. You do so if you have doubts that Spirit can achieve it, for you then begin to entertain what in essence are either counterdecrees or modifications of the original. "Is there anything too hard for the Lord?" Since you may not be able to see the steps necessary for the manifestation of your request, you may not know how near to completion it is. Practice and experience, plus always perfect faith, will teach you what and when to expect. If one plants seeds in the ground and digs them up to see if they are growing, will he reap a harvest? By experience and faith one knows they will come forth in proper sequence of operations. Loose your decrees and let them go.

Also basic in having anything done for you is the actual issue of a decree. You may wish you had many things, but until you actually turn them over to Spirit for enactment, do not expect to receive them. Do not indulge in idle dreaming and expect to have the life you should. Seeds are capable of producing the plants they represent, but they cannot do so until they are placed in the proper medium so they can be acted upon. Going back to the discussion concerning the extent of a decree: the seed, like the decree, does not do the acting; it is acted upon. So, if you want anything, and it is proper that you have it, make a decision and then release that decision to the manifesting agent always capably at your service.

IN BEST INTERESTS OF OTHERS

Regarding mention in the last sentence of your desire being proper, here is another important part of decreeing. You must be certain that fulfillment of your request is not only in your best interest but also that it in no way takes away from or is detrimental to others. In speaking of your own best interests, there are times when you may not receive what you requested. Do not think it necessarily means you have decreed improperly or are doing something wrong elsewhere. Check to see, making certain your checking does not include doubts as to eventual manifestation. Do not think Spirit will not or cannot perform. The answer may lie in your already having granted your Self the right to supersede any of your conscious decisions if they are not proper. In this case you may not receive anything; or you may receive something better in its place. Always leave the way open for your Self to take over: "Your will, not mine, be done."

As for the best interests of others, no one acting in a spiritual manner possibly could want to do or to have done anything against others; for all are part of the One. Always remember that this One will not act against Itself. If at times it seems so, it may be that one is himself in some way, directly or indirectly, responsible for seeming misfortune that befalls him. More about that later when we discuss how to prevent manifestation we do not want.

Just remember always that a prime attitude of Spirit is love; love for all creation. If this appears to be contrary to seeming destruction in nature, it is not, for what you regard as destruction is merely a rearrangement. Nothing that is real, or spiritual, ever could be destroyed; only changed in manifestation or from manifestation to nonmanifestation, which does not mean cessation of existence.

Since consideration of others is of such importance in your initiation of action, you should examine your decree in terms of how its manifestation might affect other persons. Sometimes this requires considerable analysis, for ramifications of some actions may be extensive. When you are certain it would be beneficial to all concerned or at least not be harmful or improperly limiting to others, then release it to Spirit. It would be well, in your early work, to include in your decree that no harm will come to others; later, this safeguard will not be necessary generally. Finally, if your request is not manifested in a reasonable period, check back to see if it might be due to such inherent concern to others. Just a word about checking back: do not think you will have to do so extensively or always. These suggestions refer primarily to the early stages of your spiritual development.

ADDRESS SPIRIT WITHIN YOU

In review, a point stressed early in the book is that Spirit is always where you, and all else, are. Therefore, you must not address your requests to a power far away from you, which you neither can locate nor know how to contact. Always speak, or think, to Spirit as though It were right in your thoughts, sharing them; for such is the case. All requests are deliverable at the place of your thinking: in your own consciousness.

This is true no matter what the nature of your request. It makes no difference whether the person, event or time is near at hand or distant. Your work concerns only the proper realization of the desired effect within your own consciousness. Many have believed they have things accomplished by projecting their thoughts to another person, place or time. This is not really so. Always remember that Spirit does the work; you only request it. By remembering this you will not try to project your consciousness to other places but instead will draw them into your consciousness, where you are. How do you draw them into your consciousness? Merely thinking about them already has done that.

SEE DESIRED RESULTS AS ACHIEVED

See the desired results as already achieved in your own consciousness. Do not attempt to think of them where they are and endeavor to see them changed at that location or time. Now, in your own consciousness, is the time and place for your decree and realization that it must be manifested as you have decreed. Seeing it as in the future tends to keep it in the future, since that is where you see it. Instead, see it as already accomplished within your thoughts about it, knowing that it is at that instant already established in the spiritual realm. Even if it does require what you call time to manifest, it is already in the process of such materialization. Eventually in your studies you will learn that you, too, are omnipresent in the spiritual sense, so therefore what you decree and accept in your own consciousness is effected at the corresponding physical location or time. In summary, see all things as already done in your own thoughts.

GOD IS ALL SUBSTANCE

When you come to realize that God is always present, you have arrived at a partial understanding of what is meant by His omnipresence. But believing that God is always present is not complete understanding of omnipresence, for you also must learn that God is all presence. God is all there is. This means that He is the substance of which all material is composed. It was stated earlier that Spirit is the creative force which makes as well as maintains all manifestation. It creates such manifestation by becoming what is manifested. This is why nothing manifested ever can be destroyed. Spirit merely ceases manifesting as whatever seems to be destroyed. But you do not have to understand this as yet. It is sufficient if you say all things are created of divine substance. If you are at all scientifically inclined, and thus know that all so-called physical material actually is due to particles of energy, you now may understand that this primal energy is Spirit.

Once you have learned that omnipresence means divine substance, or energy, and is the basic and only substance that exists, you see all actions and manifestations in a completely new light. You see God everywhere, as everything. You begin to realize that nothing in itself could be evil or bad, for it is all composed of Spirit. Therefore, you begin to understand that there is nothing to harm you, once you know you are one with all things. You are learning that it is man's reaction to his world, or misunderstanding of it, that causes what he calls less than perfect. You sense that you can correct these misunderstandings, completely for yourself and at least partially for others.

You understand yet more as to the manifestation of your decrees. It is not necessary for Spirit to work on inert substance that is separate from It in order to manifest anything. It creates by becoming what It is supposed to manifest. It controls manifestation by regulating Itself. Spirit is one phase of all there is: God. Thus it is not a case of your asking a God outside of your being for help, transferring that help into a decree to give to some outside force, which then acts on still other separate matter to enact your decree. All is One; different aspects, but One. If this is not clear yet, do not try to understand now; you will. For now, proceed with seeking to know and to do as you should.

TIME AND SPACE IRRELEVANT

There is no special place or time for decreeing. Do not believe you must withdraw from others or to a certain place in order to make your requests. It is true that some work may be done better where it is quiet, but this is not necessarily always true. You must learn to think properly wherever you are. Neither should you await more advantageous times of the day, year or your life for your spiritual work.

Time and space as man defines them do not exist in the spiritual realm. Time is really the succession of events, whether man regards these events as lasting for seconds or billions of years. Space is the place where these events transpire in physical manifestation. You exist in timeless and spaceless eternity as a spiritual being. Your life on Earth is but one of your infinite experiences which, since it is in a physical manifestation, is regarded by you now in terms of time and space. Learn to think and to decree properly wherever you are and whenever you should.

Unexpected bonuses will be yours as you become established more in positive thinking and proper decreeing. You will receive many things which you did not have to ask for by specific decree. You will find it less and less necessary to have to ask for the things you want or need. Jesus explained it thus: "It is your Father's good pleasure to give you the kingdom." Also, "Your Father knows that you have need of these things." Good has been prepared for us. We only must come to the place in spiritual awareness where we are able to see it and to accept it. Much of your initial decreeing will be to establish yourself in spiritual awareness. Once you have achieved it, you are free for your real work, the expression of God as your real Self. Then does life truly open to you, as you open to it.

NOTES OF CAUTION

Another note of caution: do not attempt to bring to pass that which admittedly is far beyond your comprehension or ability to use. This does not include achievement of perfect health, harmonious affairs, abundance, friends, love and others such as are expressive of your inherent nature. It does mean you should not expect to manifest immediately what you realize must require great spiritual understanding, such as materializing physical things from apparently nowhere, teleportation, or the use of abilities such as thought reading and precognition before you are ready for them.

The caution lies not in the attempt to obtain them, for you cannot

61

until you are ready, but in the possibility you may become discouraged when your lofty aspirations are not realized and therefore may abandon your studies for a while. You cannot abandon them indefinitely, for you eventually must attain, so keep at it now. Also, do not attempt to gain spiritual understanding to use selfishly. You could not obtain the true understanding but you might obtain consequences you would not want.

Proper decreeing also means you should not do so only for yourself. Many have found it easier at first to decree for others than for themselves. But whatever you do for others returns to you multiplied. You may not be able to see results of this at first, but keep at it and you will. You could not enjoy perfection if you did not help others to attain it. Advance the rate and degree of your unfoldment, and thus effectiveness of properly decreeing, by initiating helpful action for others.

Do not think that proper feeling behind a decree means that you must become highly emotional. This is far from the truth. Emotion is a good thing in its place, but its place is not in attempting to impress Spirit that you are sincere and emphatic about your decree. Emotion of a physical or mental nature is sometimes false, and sometimes a lower interpretation of a spiritual feeling. But keep it out of your decrees. Indeed, if you find such appearing when you are seeking to initiate an action, stop either the emotion or the decree, for it is not proper and could be harmful.

KEEP OUT NEGATIVE BELIEFS

In the first part of this fifth study, the effect on you of others' beliefs was mentioned. Later you read that many decrees are negative and still are enacted. Also, that the negative and error thoughts stored in memories often are more influential in our actions than the conscious positive thoughts. Add to this our oneness with all others, through Divine Mind being all there is, and you can begin to grasp the magnitude of erroneous thinking that influences you constantly, whether or not you consciously are aware of it. In order to decree properly at all times, part of your initial training is knowing about this situation and preventing it.

You have learned that you could ask your Self to act as judge on what already had accumulated; and you have benefited from this, even if you may not be yet aware of it. Also, that you could ask your Self to monitor all new ideas presented, consciously or unconsciously, to you. But still you must do much of this by your conscious self. You can begin by judging for yourself what you hear, read and see, or what has been brought to your attention in the past. One who automatically accepts without question what others tell him has no valid complaint of not knowing the truth and therefore of not being responsible. All are responsible, whether that responsibility is accepted or not.

If the information is seen to be false, discard it. If you are not certain, classify it as noneffective until you have further basis for evaluation. If it appears to be valid, accept it into your consciousness, retaining the right to reclassify it if need be. Do not be a know-it-all, a know-nothing or an indecisive and constantly changing person. No one has the right or obligation to do your thinking for you. You must learn to do it for yourself.

Be on the alert for negative suggestions in all you see and hear. Unfortunately, rather than helping man, even if this was so intentioned, much advertising has stressed negative and false conceptions that have harmed and have held back man. No talk that emphasizes man's limitations is proper. It is one thing to call attention to negative appearances and a completely different thing to set it up as a necessary or real condition. You quickly will learn what is negative and then will not allow it to register in your consciousness, no matter how often it is presented to you. But do not allow yourself to become enraged over such erroneous presentations. It will be corrected; and you can help in many quietly effective ways, rather than upsetting yourself and others.

However, do not overdo this searching out of negative influences, for you then would tend to bring more of them to bear upon you. Pass judgment upon and admit or reject those which come to your attention. Soon you will have little need to concern yourself with being influenced in this manner. But do not forget that still you must judge what is presented to your consciousness. It is just that you need not be on guard against subtle negative influences to the same extent.

As for others deliberately attempting to harm you, there will be no actual danger unless you either expect it or allow it to occur. So long as you think and act in accord with divine love, you cannot be harmed by any person, thing or event; unless you have invited it through action of the law of cause and effect, and even then much can be transmuted. This may seem hard to believe at first, but you soon will come to know it is so. Your radiation of divine love sets at naught all harmful intentions toward you. Anyone persisting in such attempts has only himself to blame for consequences to him. Always recognize and salute the real Self of others. Recognize Spirit as the only power there is and nothing harmful can befall you. Of course, this has referred only to improper intentions against you. Proper thoughts and decrees by others on your behalf still will benefit you.

This fifth study is longer than the previous ones because it dwells mainly on the work you are to do in achieving the degree of spiritual awareness that will permit you to act in your real nature. What came before was preparatory understanding necessary for this step. What follows is based on this study effectively having been put into practice. As this increasingly is done, you decreasingly are concerned with overcoming improper thinking and decreeing and are more capable of acting in your spiritual nature.

▲

6. FIVE DEGREES OF INITIATING DIVINE ACTION

YOU ARE AN EXPRESSER OF GOD

You are an expression of God in this world, this system of things. This description of you certainly is worth consideration. It means the same if it is rearranged to say you are God expressing in this system of things. Do not permit anyone to make a play on words and thereby cause you to fall short of your rightful place. Does it really change anything to say that God, who is all, expresses through you; or to say that you are a representative of God in this world? Nor can refusal to accept this reality change it in the eternal scheme of things.

The difficulty, and therefore the need for spiritual awakening and growth, is that we came into this world not knowing of our divinity. As infants we were not even aware of what we were. It took several years before we knew ourselves to be humans. Much of humanity even then knew no further identity. When we learned of a power greater than human, we were told many things, depending on the groups into which we were born. Most of us were taught that this supreme power is separate from us.

We probably were taught that there are one or more additional powers operating against the supreme power. Even Christians are taught that although God is omnipotent, the only power, there is an evil power called Satan. This is a paradox. If there is only one power, how can there also be another power? Man as a whole failed to understand that theologists built up this myth of an adversary by mistaking the biblical meaning, which refers to the adverse thinking of man himself. Thereby much of mankind has been held in baseless fear of an evil power, and thus God's lack of omnipotence. Of course, the concept of a devil made it easy to attempt to shift responsibility for man's own mistakes. However, the attempt was to no avail, for man still reaped what he sowed or did not prevent from being harvested.

Now mankind is becoming increasingly aware of his inherent spiritual nature. The time will come when children will know this with the same surety they now know they are human. There will be no need of teachers to tell them who and what they are, for "I will put my laws into their mind, and write them in their hearts . . . and they shall not teach every man his neighbor . . . for all shall know me, from the least to the greatest."

Meanwhile, following in the footsteps of the spiritually illumined of many eons, you now have the opportunity to achieve this awareness and to "Let your light so shine before men that they may see your good works and glorify your Father which is in the heavens." As you thus reveal God to others, they will be inspired to learn and to do in similar manner. It is not necessary that one do the same works, or even great works, in order to ignite the spiritual spark in others. For Self in you greets Self in others, and each personal self becomes more aware.

As for the works performed in spiritual awareness, no credit is taken by the personal self; for the personal self becomes more and more the real Self, which is the true source of both the ideas and the manifestation of the ideas. Or, in other words, you know you act as an expresser of God in such works. You know you are the means whereby the infinite expresses in the finite. As man you are able to function both in the infinite and the finite.

In this capacity you are able to turn to the infinite for ideas and then to turn back to the finite both to bring them into physical manifestation and to enjoy those manifestations. The purpose of life is to live and to bring forth that life for ever more abundant living. Did not the Self in Jesus say, "I am come that they might have life, and that they might have it more abundantly"? Does this coincide with various religious ideas which have taught that man must lead a bare existence, devoid of the pleasure of living? Certainly not, so do not permit yourself to be bound by beliefs that deny life the right to express more fully through you. Express life properly, which includes bringing forth life as creation. Live and enjoy life. You will not be able to express much, though, if you improperly limit the type or degree of expression.

Your unfoldment now consists of learning how to receive divine ideas so you may put to use your power to decree, and thus to bring them into physical and mental existence for the enjoyment of God as you and others. Why is it necessary to bring them into manifestation? Do you receive as much enjoyment from just thinking about what would be pleasant as you do from actually physically enjoying it? Does your just thinking about it help others to use it? Then, manifestation.

For this purpose have you learned of your spiritual nature and how to live it. You learn to become your Self. Then do you know and accomplish the purposes for which you are. Are what? Just are. What do you want to be and to do? Just decree it, in your spiritual consciousness, and you are. Do not attempt too firmly to establish this, what you want to be and to do, until you can do so with spiritual understanding, for with that understanding you see things altogether differently. This does not mean you should do nothing or set no goals meanwhile; it merely means you may want to change them.

How do you learn to receive God's ideas? By now there should be no hesitation in answering: ask Spirit to do the teaching. You will be led to those who can help teach you, both in person and through their works. Even those who may not seem to qualify as either teachers or students of the spiritual can be sources through which Spirit teaches you. Many times, apparently unrelated events will reveal the information. Or you may seem to receive ideas as by chance, although you will know it is not chance. Nothing happens by chance or coincidence for the spiritually aware. You may not be aware consciously that it was about to happen or how it happened, but you know it was done by Spirit.

COMMUNING WITH GOD

All of these and more are used by Spirit to bring ideas to you for recognition and action. But it is also necessary that you learn how to commune directly with God. Not only will you want to seek ideas for manifestation but also you will seek to know more about God, His wisdom, His companionship and His plans. At times you will wish to rest in infinite contemplation. For many reasons, including that of becoming your Self, you must learn to be one with God consciously.

To do this you are going to receive but little additional information here. This is done deliberately, not because it is unknown or unexperienced but because this communion must be a personal thing with you. No one else can share this communion with you or achieve it in exactly the manner you do. You already have been given all the information you need, but a few aids will be added. Do not try to follow any other's method exactly. You are an individual.

First, you must wish to commune with God directly. You must at least admit the possibility of such communion. Do not think you are unworthy of being in God's presence, for you always have been in His presence. Do not think of communing with the infinite on a finite level. Rather than thinking of God as coming down to the finite level of consciousness to commune with you, think of yourself expanding into infinite consciousness to meet Him.

Try to withdraw from outside activity as much as possible during these periods. Free your thoughts as much as you can from outer things. Have these periods regularly, of varying intervals and often. Think of yourself as always in His presence, not only during these communions but at all times. Begin these periods with praise and thanksgiving. Seek various results in different periods: oneness, rest, information, happiness, love, or whatever else you would like to experience or to know. Conclude each communion with loving thanks.

MEDITATION EXPERIENCES

Do not expect consciously to be aware of His presence always, and especially at first. However, do not expect not to be so aware. Sometimes you may receive the desired result immediately, at other times you may receive it later. Do not expect to see God in human form. Do not expect to hear or to see anything. Although after a while you may experience, with your eyes closed, visual and audible scenes as in dreams or daydreams, do not think this is necessary.

You may experience the reception of understanding and ideas in the nature of intuitive flashes. You may have the sensation of thinking about something, yet knowing you could not possibly be consciously thinking it yourself. In such experiences the entire thought sequence may last only a matter of what you call seconds, yet you are aware it would take you perhaps hours to run through exactly the same sequence. Or you may experience a period that best can be described as just knowing. This state is beyond thinking. As you progress in spiritual attainment, you will do less thinking as reasoning and more thinking from knowing.

MEDITATION PURPOSES

There are times when you will wish specific knowledge in answer to some particular problem. You may not receive any conscious answer but the problem will be solved. Or you may receive your answer by means of a thought seemingly just coming to you from nowhere when you are doing or thinking of something else. Often you block the answer by too much concentration on trying to get it. Familiarity with scriptures is most helpful, for often your answer will be revealed by means of a passage coming to your attention, setting off a chain of thoughts. Other illumined writings will serve the same purpose.

There also are times when you should not seek specific information but should ask that you be made aware of what God wishes you to know. These can be periods of outstanding illumination, often bringing you understanding of things you would not have thought about. You may experience pure at-onement that takes you completely out of awareness of time and space and into the state of knowing your Self as just being. Once this has happened, you never again will have any doubt about your eternal nature. You know you always exist because in Spirit there is no time or space, unless so desired. Being in this state does not mean being unconscious to everything; only to manifestation.

But do not return from even this high experience with a desire to be done with this world; for you are here for a purpose, otherwise you would not be here. It must be important, so look upon contact with both the infinite and the finite in anticipation of many pleasures from all phases of life.

An idea for manifestation is the image of or pattern for the completed creation. In order to become that manifestation, the idea must be transformed from the spiritual to the mental and physical realms. In other words, ideas of themselves do not accomplish any more than do seeds of themselves. You must act on the ideas you receive from God. The ideas may be presented to you before you have received sufficient understanding to know how to interpret them or how to bring them forth. But if you received the idea from Divine Mind, at the proper time you also will receive the understanding and the means to bring it forth.

Make certain you consider the idea carefully. Many rush forth with an incomplete or an improper analysis of an idea and bring forth confusion. It may require great patience to hold an idea for what seems to you considerable time. But the idea was not yours in the first place, so learn patience. Remember that God and His spiritual realm are eternal. What man considers as passing of time is only a limited glimpse of eternity. Although it is well to consider divine ideas carefully, it is still necessary to know how to initiate the action of Spirit to bring the ideas into manifestation.

Decree is the general term used in this book, although *request, want, prayer, affirmation, command, visualization* and *realization* also have been employed. Though the various words have different meanings, they were used previously in the general sense of the initiation of Spirit's action. Let us examine some of these terms in the form of degrees of understanding and thus of effective use in initiating action. This is not a differentiation you are apt to find elsewhere, but you will find it more flexible and, as you progress, less limiting than many of the previously used methods of only one or several of these. The terms in themselves are not new; only the differentiation in meaning of degree.

THE FIVE DEGREES

In order of use in increasing spiritual awareness, the five degrees are: denial and affirmation, affirmation, decree, visualization, and realization. There is no complete change from one to another in the sense of eliminating one as you pass on to the use of the next. Not only does your need vary depending on the situation but you grow by a gradual process rather than in distinct steps. Also, you will have occasion to use even the fundamental step as you help others along the way. Actually, each classification describes the method you use predominantly in a certain stage of your growth. Even when you utilize mainly realization, you occasionally will use even denial and affirmation, in addition to the others. It will not be any problem to decide which method to use; you will know automatically.

It may seem at times that saying you will know what to do is actually an admission of lack of knowledge or of withholding such knowledge, but this is not the reason. Not only does each person differ because each is an individual but the purpose of this book is not to be all-inclusive. It is only a guide to contacting the teacher within you. It is this teacher, Spirit, who will instruct you, as you permit. In this respect you are essentially the one who must give permission; essentially, but not entirely and inevitably.

DENIAL AND AFFIRMATION

Denial and affirmation is the preliminary process which is needed to eliminate error ideas that have been stored in your consciousness. Since your actions, including what has happened to you, are caused by the ideas you hold, it is necessary that you discard those ideas which cause what you do not want and substitute those which will give you what you do want. That is the reason for this first process.

Until you are well into one phase, do not try too hard to master a higher phase. You will not be able to master any step until you have understood and have used the preceding steps. You will be made aware of your readiness for advancement. It is a matter of training both what are called the conscious and the subconscious.

In the beginning, just because you consciously agree with an idea that is new to you does not mean you have eliminated a false idea on the same subject from your memory. Fortunately it is not that easy, for if it were you would be changing your beliefs constantly, often without your conscious awareness. So, proceed in proper order from

71

the beginning; you cannot do otherwise, anyhow. But you could slow or stop your progress without having known why.

Denial is the first part of the first step because you must deny wrong ideas any right to a place in your consciousness. These may be ideas put there by you or by past experiences of others. In the fifth study you learned how to obtain the necessary assistance of Spirit in denying and thus eliminating many of the false beliefs. You also were told how to recognize those ideas which would be presented to you for conscious judgment. And you were alerted to the denying or affirming of ideas or beliefs that come to you daily.

Do not expect to be able to deny out of your memory all false beliefs immediately. Not only would it be impossible but it would be such a tremendous mental shock that possibly you would not be able to stand it. So much of what we have believed to be true is actually only partially true or completely false that you might soon be in a state of utter bewilderment, not knowing what to believe. Consequently, Spirit will guide the process so you will not be overwhelmed. But as you begin to emerge from the early and greatest part of the denial period, you will be joyous and thrilled at the glorious real world all about you that you never before even imagined.

This explanation has been included so you would not be alarmed at any seeming turmoil which might cause you to abandon your work. It is the inner meaning of the events leading up to and ending in the War of Armageddon in the New Testament; the last battle between your right and wrong beliefs and the wondrous new heaven that comes to you after you have won the battle, which you most certainly will if you persist.

Therefore, denial must precede acceptance of new beliefs concerning those subjects on which you already have beliefs. When you do not have already entrenched false beliefs, then affirmation or acceptance alone is sufficient. Since you cannot hold wrong beliefs on any idea and still expect to make a true analysis and decision, the false must go. Not only must they go so you can effect proper action but also that you no longer experience the undesirable things they cause by being a part of your collective thinking.

The error thoughts which are embedded firmly may require considerable emphatic work on your part in order to cast out those devils or adverse thoughts. There may be times when it seems certain thoughts have acquired a thinking power of their own to mock, to torment and to threaten you. This seeming power is only that which you have placed in those thoughts. Take back that power and watch how fast they disappear.

Various religions state that a man's worst enemies are those of his own household. Those enemies are your error thoughts, and your household is your consciousness. You are master of that household. You can and must deny residence therein to any enemy thought. If you do not seem to have enough strength to cast out certain demon thoughts, remember, "The battle is not yours, but God's." Ask the help of your Self. Then, "Fear not, stand still and see the salvation of Jehovah."

But, for a large part of this elimination, denial is only half the process. Most of us have had so much of our consciousness based upon partial and complete error ideas that if all were to be eliminated, with true ideas not being substituted, we would be as a barren house. Jesus used just such an analogy in the story of the man who cast out a demon which, upon returning and finding the house swept clean and empty, went to bring back other demons, making the plight of that man worse than before. This story illustrates what happens if we consciously do not replace negative with positive thinking.

Man is a thinking being and it is seldom that he is able to still his thoughts completely. He can think for himself or let others do most of it for him, but by his very nature thoughts are usually passing through his consciousness. If, like the man in the story, we sweep out all negative thoughts and do not fill our mental household with positive thoughts, the old and also new negative thoughts will flow in, making our condition worse than before. Therefore, we must not replace error ideas with the right ideas alone but we also constantly must increase our understanding by adding new truths. It cannot be a halfway process.

In making use of the denial and affirmation method, whether for yourself, for others or for any other purpose, you first deny what you have believed previously or what seems to be wrong. This denial is actually convincing yourself that no longer are you to believe as right what you are now saying is wrong. Next you affirm or tell yourself what the truth of the matter is. At first you may find it helpful to do this by writing or speaking aloud both the denial and the affirmation. This aids in impressing your consciousness.

You may have to repeat it at intervals, but do not dwell on it too much. You will learn later that as you progress in your power of speaking the word, the tendency to emphasize the negative will serve to manifest it. The important point is to remember that you are training your entire consciousness to accept and to act according to your inherent spiritual nature of having the power to initiate the action of Spirit by use of your thoughts.

Spirit, through your subconscious, is impressed by the meaning and feeling behind your words, not by the words themselves. Ten million people may speak exactly the same words in an attempt to initiate spiritual action, yet only one may be successful. Why? He knows, his entire consciousness knows and motivating force knows that he is aware of his spiritual nature and the attendant powers, and that because he says it will be done it is to be done. This is what you too can and must achieve. "You also shall decree a thing, and it shall be established unto you"; and "So shall my word be that goes forth out of my mouth: it shall not return unto me void, but it shall accomplish that which I please, and it shall prosper in the thing whereto I send it."

But you must believe fully and use this; just knowledge accomplishes nothing. "Faith without works is dead." So, do not be concerned too much over the words or the method of saying them, as long as they contain the desirable information. Seek instead to maintain complete, sincere and emphatic faith in what you are doing. Furthermore, believe that your words already have accomplished that for which they were spoken.

AFFIRMATION

The second level of speaking the word is affirmation. To a limited extent, you are capable of using affirmation alone in the beginning, when you are adding ideas to your consciousness which are not hampered by any error thoughts. When there is no false belief to deny, there is no need to use denial. In such cases you do not want

74

to believe such and such because you do want to believe something else.

However, affirmation alone is a method you could use only sparingly at first, because of the wide scope and intricately interwoven, often untraceable or undetectable, nature of less than true ideas you have held about so many things. But the more you use denial, the less you have to deny, therefore the more use of affirmation alone. As you progress you have fewer improper thoughts to eliminate and to guard against and more proper ones to add. Remember, do not throw out the worthless and fail to add the worthwhile. As you grow, be it physically or mentally or spiritually, you have more room for added things. Utilize that expansion properly.

Both denial and affirmation, and affirmation alone are more for the purpose of setting things right than for higher accomplishments. This is another limiting factor when one fails to see or to move on to a higher form. Affirming something to be accomplished is not the same as decisively instructing that it be accomplished. One may be achieving higher demonstrations through what he calls affirmation, but closer analysis would reveal actual use of a more advanced method.

But do not be too impatient to advance. It is most important that your advancement be tempered with assimilation of what you have learned. Therefore, note this: when you reach a period where it seems you no longer are progressing, or even seem to have fallen back, know that it is only a period of absorbing what you have learned. Instead of despairing or thinking you may have done something terribly wrong, for which your goal is being denied you, give thanks while enjoying and using what you already have. At the same time, look forward to the truly wondrous things to happen, beyond your present comprehension. This advance notice, as those preceding, is for the purpose of preventing alarm, fear or confusion that otherwise might slow or stop your spiritual unfoldment. Having been called to your conscious attention already, they will lessen or will prevent such hindrance, for so it has been directed.

The third level is that of the decree. While the first two levels may be thought of as essentially preparatory training, the third may be regarded as the stage of putting that training to work. With the decree, you cannot obtain much until you really understand and believe your spiritual power. However, do not refrain from exploratory attempts to use it early in your training, so long as you know that failure to obtain results consistently does not mean it is an invalid concept. The rate of unfoldment varies tremendously with the individual, so there is no set schedule which everyone should follow. Allow your Self to guide you as to when you are ready to begin advanced study.

As more attain spiritual awareness, those who follow will find it easier and quicker. Thus, while one who began fifty years ago may have attained a certain level in ten years, one who started twenty years ago may have reached a similar peak in five years, and one now beginning may do it in a year or even a few months. There are many reasons why this is so: there were comparatively few who even had heard of, let alone attained, this understanding until the latter nineteenth century; much of the trial-and-error work has been accomplished by those who preceded; many race error thoughts have been weakened considerably by the work of those who have achieved spiritual awareness; much more information and instruction are now openly available; there are varying degrees of interest, present aptitude and available time for study among those who are now beginning; and many old or advanced souls had mastered these subjects in previous lives.

Therefore, do not hesitate to experiment a little and to let your pace be set primarily by your Self. You may be required to follow a certain schedule if you train for spiritual work with a specific organization, but there you should find no restriction against additional study of your own. Actually, the more you rely on God to guide you, the faster you will unfold. This does not mean He will not lead you to make use of other instructors and material, but much unnecessary work will be eliminated.

An affirmation is an assertion that something exists or is true.

A decree is an authoritative order. These are dictionary definitions and serve to show the difference between the first two levels and the third. It also may be phrased another way, showing that the former is an acceptance and the latter is an issuance. The affirmation states what is established, the decree directs what is to be established. One enters more into the authoritative, yet humble, active state of initiating requests for fulfillment by Spirit as he passes beyond the passive training state of accepting his spiritual heritage. But the initial training was necessary so he could convince himself, and thus Creative Energy, that he had the right and the duty to follow the Old Testament directive: "Thus says the Lord . . . concerning the work of my hands, command me."

When decreeing you must be certain it is proper, as discussed earlier. Before stating the decree make certain, at least until you fully have established faith in your ability, that you are functioning in the spiritual state of consciousness. Preface the decree with a statement that you speak these words in the Self consciousness, even though at the time you may not be aware of any change in consciousness. Have an attitude not of brash boldness but of rightfully expecting the cooperation of the perfect partner. This process of requesting by you and performing by Spirit is just that: divine cooperation between phases of Divine Mind; you the dispenser of divine decrees and Spirit the creating agent.

State the decree as clearly as possible, showing that you know what you wish accomplished. Phrase it not as something to be established but as something that already has been established because you are so decreeing. The real establishment is created in the spiritual realm with the issuance of the decree, while the manifestation is the establishment in the physical realm. Always remember that all creation is first accomplished in thought; the physical creation follows. Spiritual cause produces physical effect. Once it is established in the spiritual, the physical manifestation must follow, providing the spiritual cause is not altered or not canceled. Again, it is necessary that you believe your request already is granted on the spiritual and therefore it must manifest, regardless of what the mental or physical appearance might be.

Do not try to instruct Spirit how to accomplish the manifestation.

This is often hard for one to keep from doing at first, but it is important that you do not attempt to limit the manner in which Spirit is to work. Spirit is all-knowing in the ways of creation, while man certainly is not. The manifestation may come about in what one might call a normal manner, but it also may be accomplished in an unexpected and inconceivably amazing manner. Unless your decree is for a specific thing, do not make it so exact that something better or more abundant is prevented from appearing. You can allow for this by including the idea of "This, or something better, as You wish."

Make your attitude one of gratitude. Feel love for Spirit. Give thanks that it has been done. Additional thanks and praise certainly would not be amiss. You would not hesitate to express love, praise and thanks for much less done by a loved one. And you certainly will not express these feelings to God only when you are asking for something. Finally, in ending your decree you may find it helpful to emphasize, for your own benefit, its establishment by adding "So be it."

VISUALIZATION

Visualization is the fourth degree. There is no dividing line between the three highest degrees; it is more a gradual evolving. The chief distinction between decreeing and visualization is the degree of your recognition of your right to use this power of initiating action by Spirit. This includes practice and experimentation, greater faith due to many successful decreeings, and increased spiritual understanding.

In practice it is the elimination of the preparation and of the issuance of a formal decree. You just think of the desired manifestation and know that because you are thinking of it as a visualization, it will be manifested. You might compare decreeing and visualizing in this manner: a visualization is an idea not expressed in words, while a decree is an idea that is converted into words. Thus, in the visualization it is not necessary to convey your request into words.

It is an erroneous concept which states that man can think only by words. It is true that much of the time this is so, but in such experiences as enjoying a sunset or receiving an idea that is new to the world, the thinking is in terms of picturing, or even pure knowing, rather than words. As in the enjoyment of the sunset, you may have feelings concerning the scene but you do not attempt to convert the sunset or your feelings into words. Actually, pure thought precedes every creation; and creation includes words. This brief denial has been included so you will not be prevented from advancing to the higher spiritual levels of visualization and realization by this limiting error belief.

You will not be able to achieve what you believe to be impossible. Never allow yourself to be limited by what others may think is impossible. Either use your own imagination or reserve judgment. It is not necessary that you have an opinion on any point until you can decide competently; you can be neutral. A wrong idea can limit you and prevent advancement, whereas no opinion about an idea may not.

Since there is no formal preparation of your request in visualization, or in realization, there is not much in the nature of specific instruction. You will do most of your early work in this stage along the lines of what you have had the most experience in decreeing. This is because you will have seen sufficient manifestations caused by your decrees to know that further requests surely will follow. As this happens you will have a natural tendency to save the time and effort required to think a formal decree. However, you still may use decrees in other instances, where you are not yet sure you are advanced enough to use visualization or in fields new to you. But as you become more assured that visualization can and does work, you will use it increasingly.

It would be well to note now that as you progress through these stages, you will have increasing opportunities to use this power of initiating action. You will discover many needs to be fulfilled. These needs, of wide variety, will be brought to your attention in many ways, some of them causing you to be thrilled with amazement, humility, understanding and other feelings. You may be annoyed at a situation that delays or inconveniences you, only to find that it caused you to be in the right place at the right time to help someone, or to initiate or to prevent an action. A practice that will enhance greatly your usefulness, and thence your understanding, is to say, each morning before you arise, that you are at the disposal of Spirit to do whatever you can to be of service.

One more consideration: there will be times when you realize that God has directed you to a situation so you can have something done about it. You may wonder why you were called upon to cause it to be done. Could not He have done it directly? Do it and ponder on it later, for there was a reason. Somewhat similar in nature to this is when you are given the idea that your speaking of the word would be effective in a field you never would have dreamed possible. These are intensely thrilling experiences. Live up to such trusts.

REALIZATION

The fifth degree is realization. To initiate action in this stage of awareness, you have only to observe that a situation is not manifesting as it should; it will be corrected. Or you have only to notice a need; it will be met. Whatever you realize should be, will be. You need make no conscious effort to initiate action; your observation of or about anything is sufficient. Perhaps classifiable in realization or perhaps a higher step, it makes no difference in this discussion, is never coming into the presence of any lasting error condition; one's very presence corrects the condition. This only is mentioned here, nothing more. Neither is there anything else to be said of realization here; you will learn directly when you are able to receive it.

SPIRITUAL ADVANCEMENT

From even this brief discussion of at least five degrees of your use of spiritual power, you can see there is much to learn. This has been concerned only with your ability to initiate spiritual action. There are other phases of spiritual unfoldment, such as understanding the nature of God, yourself and all creation; learning and aiding the purposes of creation; enjoying your ever-expanding consciousness; increasing associations with others who are discovering and living the real life; new interests, and the helping of others.

So, there is no lack of understandings for you to acquire and no lack of applications for you to utilize and to enjoy. Be persistent as you begin and soon you will be carried forward with little or no further need for self-persistence. Once you get into the Spirit of things, you will have enough Spirit to do all things.

Your spiritual advancement depends not only on what you receive but also on what you give. It is a law that you must give of what you have in order to receive more. You will discover, or perhaps already have discovered, that the more you give of spiritual gifts, the more you will have to give. As a divine expression, an expresser of God, you are to express or to press out divine gifts and works, to co-operate in their manifestation in this world.

Do not be concerned if your works often go unnoticed or unappreciated; think of what God does without insisting upon man's notice or thanks. But whatsoever you do for anyone or anything will not go unnoticed by your real Self. It will repay you manyfold in many ways, for we all are part of the One.

You have done well in learning of your eternal spiritual nature. You will do well in learning how to manifest your real Self. You will do well to assist others to do the same. You will do well to express and to enjoy life. You will do well to know all is well. So it is. Welcome to life!

▲

II. 100 SPIRITUAL TRUTHS

It is of no value to hear that you must change ideas unless you know which need changing to what. Neither are they of practical value to you until you have been able to incorporate them in your own consciousness and use. Nor are one's ideas of any value if he either condemns ideas without substituting right ones or does not live up to his own suggestions. It is well to test, by use as well as analysis, ideas which have been proved by others until you have seen enough proof yourself to take ideas from those sources on faith without having to prove each one. Much unnecessary work can be eliminated in this manner. But be certain you do not follow blindly without adequate initial proof that it is the positive path which leads to spiritual freedom and not the negative path which leads to mortal bondage.

Paradoxical as it may seem, those who offer negative ideas have proved them to work, at least in their lives. It has been said that even this bringing forth of negative fruit is proof of man's divinity; for it proves his ability to create, by having created, whatever he decrees. Jesus told us we can know others by the fruit they bring forth. He did not say only positive fruit or no fruit could be brought forth. Therefore, be yourself the judge of the fruit you wish to bring forth. If negative, follow those ideas and remain dead. If positive, follow these ideas and be born into life.

This section has been included so you may learn of some true ideas that are necessary for entry into spiritual consciousness and action. They are not in any sense new, for truth is eternally the same. Nor is this the first they have been called forth to man's attention. But the important time for you is when you first know and use them. Since truth never need argue its case, no attempt is made here to prove anything. One who sincerely wants truth will have it revealed to him; one who does not want proof usually will not need to worry about getting it. Give these ideas the opportunity to be proved in your life. They are few in number here but they will lead you to many others. Ask God within to make you aware of truth. He always will, if you but learn to listen and to accept what you hear.

1. THE BASIS OF EVERYTHING

God is.

2. REALITY AND APPEARANCE

The spiritual realm is the true reality. When the mental and physical exactly coincide with spiritual realities, they also are real. When they do not, they are not real but conditional. Realities are actual, conditions are factual. Perfection is reality, imperfection is conditional. Imperfection is a condition that seems real but which in reality either is not imperfection or does not exist. It can be real but called imperfect due to lack of complete understanding of it. It does not exist in reality if it has been imagined or has been brought forth by man's imperfect creating.

Because something has no basis in reality does not mean it does not exist for man or that he is not affected by such conditions. Man's five outer senses are established to record a certain range of manifestation. Additional aids extend that range. Mental faculties assess these reports. Such assessments may be based on incomplete or inexact reports. The intellect may base conclusions on physical observations alone or may make mental adjustments before reaching conclusions. Either or both the physical and mental observations may be inexact or incomplete. Conclusions based upon such observations may cause man to seem to see imperfection. Effects caused by impersonal workings of natural laws may seem imperfect when man judges them in personal relationship to himself.

3. PERFECTION AND IMPERFECTION

In reality there is neither perfection nor imperfection. All that exists in the spiritual realm just is. Even perfection is a limiting definition in that it implies a comparison to imperfection, which is not a spiritual possibility. Therefore, by the use of the term *perfect* to describe a spiritual reality, it must be remembered that it is only a method of comparison with what seems to man as less than perfect or less than what it should be. The same applies to the use of any term used to describe reality, such as *good, love, health* and *peace*. This is the meaning of saying that something just is, because any attempt to define it would limit it either by thinking of its opposite or by expressing only some of its attributes. This particularly applies when speaking about God.

4. OMNIPRESENCE

God is Omnipresence. His is the only presence, regardless of man's seeming to see many of different types. He is the only substance, regardless of appearances of many.

5. OMNISCIENCE

God is Omniscience. His is the only Mind. Man has consciousness in, and thus use of, Divine Mind; as much as he comprehends and uses. Divine Mind knows all things. Divine Mind is able to provide all information and ideas and to solve all problems. God is the source of all understanding.

6. OMNIPOTENCE

God is Omnipotence. He is the only power. Man has use of divine power as he is able to understand and to direct it. God can do all things with no effort. God as power does all things. As man more fully understands this, he sees that he of himself does nothing, but has all things done for him. The more he knows and applies this, the less he thinks it necessary for him to labor mentally and physically.

7. NO REAL DEVIL

There is no such identity as Satan the devil. This false idea is due to mistaken interpretation of scriptural references to man's own adverse thinking and to false gods. It has been fostered and has been maintained deliberately by many churches to hold man in fear of God so as to force religions on him.

8. NO REAL HELL

There is no such specific region as hell. It is a state of consciousness held by man. It is due to improper thoughts that seem to make his living miserable. Since he either places himself in or does not leave that consciousness, man makes his own hell. Even though from the outer this may not seem true always, the condition is one of mental and physical appearance only. As a spiritual being, man is always in the real state of heaven. He has but to know this and to turn there in thought. The mental and physical states will come to correspond.

9. NO REAL FEAR

Fear does not exist in reality, the spiritual realm. There could be nothing to fear, for all is love, and nothing happens by chance.

10. GOD DOES NOT CAUSE FEAR

God neither causes nor wishes man to fear Him. Apparent scriptural references to such fearing are due to mistaken interpretation of intention. To hold in awe better conveys the meaning. Man created fear and must eliminate its unrealities.

11. GOD GIVES ONLY GOOD

God is good. Man should not attempt to justify his unfortunate experiences by saying God caused them for man's own good, for such is not so. Good cannot be less than good.

12. GOD DOES NOT PUNISH

God does not punish. God has established divine laws. These natural laws are impersonal. Man's attempts to violate these laws result in the consequences he mistakenly calls punishment. Ignorance of these laws does not set them aside.

13. DIVINE LOVE AND DIVINE LAW

God is love. Divine love cannot think or cannot act in any manner except love. There can be no exceptions. If man believes love could not permit apparent suffering, he does not understand that all is love and yet all is law. Love cannot set aside law, for divine law is changeless. Through understanding of love and law, man can change conditions so no inharmony results.

Man has free will. It takes a great love to allow one to learn how to exercise his powers without interfering. There are times when one should be helped and times when he should not be helped. Some guides are: when he asks for help, when he learns from such help, when he is being dangerously or improperly treated by another, when he is doing or about to do serious harm to himself, and when one receives divine impulse to help.

14. GOD SHOWS NO FAVORITISM

God is impartial. Divine love does not play favorites. Divine law is impersonal and cannot be variable. It is pointless to ask for special favor over anyone, regardless of the other's actions. Learn to act according to natural laws and you will need no special favors. The policy of asking for God's favor over anyone, for any purpose, is presumptuous ignorance.

15. DIVINE AND HUMAN LOVE

Divine love does not mean approval of improper action. The spiritually aware love all other persons, as well as all other creations. However, this does not mean they necessarily like the way others are thinking and acting. Divine love recognizes the spiritual Self within each person, and can do so while disliking the personal self that is acting contrary to his inherent spiritual nature. This is the meaning of loving all people; divine love as distinguished from human love.

16. GOD JUDGES NO ONE

God judges no one. Divine creations are perfect and need no further judgment than "And God saw everything that He had made, and behold, it was very good." This includes man. It is only man acting in less than spiritual awareness who judges. Those who know better understand they should "Judge not, that you be not judged." "For with what judgment you judge, you shall be judged." You really only can judge yourself. It is one thing to judge another's actions but quite another to judge him.

17. DIVINE UNDERSTANDING
RATHER THAN FORGIVING

God never has to forgive, for He understands why man acts as he does. Improper actions are only the result of not knowing better. This is so no matter how deliberate the actions may be. If one truly were aware of his spiritual nature, he would not act improperly. Man has been created perfect and therefore he is already perfect, in the spiritual realm.

Man does not function accordingly always in the mental and physical realms while he is still in the process of attaining that perfection. Thus do the spiritually aware see him, as one who is following the inner urge toward perfection. However, no matter how perfect the idea he senses, he cannot interpret it any higher than he is able to understand it. Therefore, his actions are interpreted in that light. There is need not for forgiveness but for understanding and love.

18. NECESSITY OF UNDERSTANDING
AND FORGIVING

Forgiveness is necessitated by man's action and therefore is capable of being granted by man. One must never withhold either understanding or forgiveness for any thoughts or actions of others toward him, for he himself cannot be forgiven completely if he does. The judge in the reckoning is one's own superconscious. One must seek some form of forgiveness for his improper acts. Although one who knows how may cause some of another's mistakes to be forgiven, each person is the only one who can forgive himself completely. Everyone has this power and must exercise it. Remember, God understands man's actions, man forgives them.

19. MISTAKES CANNOT AFFECT GOD

A sin is not an offense against God. It is not within man's power to offend, to wrong or to harm God. A sin is a mistake. It is a missing of the mark, a failure to live up to the spiritual nature. Man can only commit such mistakes or sins against himself, other men and other physical manifestations. He cannot affect wrongly the spiritual realm of reality in any way whatsoever.

20. SIN AND PUNISHMENT ACTUALLY WORKING OF LAW OF CAUSE AND EFFECT

Mistakes, erroneously called sins, are thoughts and actions contrary to natural laws. Neither God nor the laws punish man for such mistakes; man's actions bring about certain results. This is known as the law of cause and effect. Man's basic use of forgiveness is a giving for: for a mistaken cause that gives a wrong effect, he gives a proper cause for a right effect. *Forgive* means *to give for.*

21. ELIMINATING EFFECTS OF MISTAKES

Man is under bondage to mistakes or sins only until they have been forgiven by himself or others. Forgiveness completely erases them and they no longer are held against one. God never did hold them against one; the law of cause and effect caused it to be so manifested. When a new effect is established, the old one is canceled and the new one so instituted will lead to another effect. Of course, mistakes of major proportion may require that equally major proper causes be substituted for them. But the effect holds only until a new effect has taken its place. There is no divine or eternal judgment of punishment held against one.

22. MEANING OF ORIGINAL SIN

There is no such thing as being born under original sin in the sense that some religions have misconstrued it. Man's original sin is thinking of himself as separate from the Christ within, believing he has an existence away from, or in spite of, or in addition to the Spirit that is within all of us equally. There is no separation and can be no separation. All of man's sins are those created from his thinking he is separate from God.

23. RELIGION SERVES MAN

No person or group has any valid spiritual claim on anyone. They may act as guides and aids, but they could not have any possible spiritual claim over anyone else. They can and do serve man well, but man is not made to be subservient to them. They may be able to exercise undue restraint on man in the mental and physical, but cannot do so in the spiritual. This includes all religious groups. As mankind now hastens ever more rapidly to spiritual unfoldment, any such attempts to bind will lead to the weakening of that which would bind.

24. SYMBOLS HAVE NO POWER

Symbols of any kind are effective only insofar as their meaning is known to the user. They have no effect on man's outer consciousness unless he understands them. This is necessarily true whether he uses them or they are used for him. Do not use specific symbols when you have passed the stage of need for them. Symbols here include rites.

25. CHARMS AND GOOD-LUCK PIECES HAVE NO POWER

Charms have no value in themselves, be they good-luck pieces or religious items. All such things are superstitious graven images which seek to incur favor from or through some supposed power less than God. He needs no such affronts to invoke His aid, for He is always instantly accessible to man in his own thoughts. The statement that such items actually are not prayed or spoken to as such, but only act as reminders, is not necessarily valid. Usually they really are thought to contain powers, or they deliberately are forced on man to cause him to believe he needs a mediator between God and him. The more burdens laid on man, the harder it is for him to become free.

26. NO ONE CAN TAKE AWAY MAN'S SPIRITUAL HERITAGE

No group in any way whatsoever can deny you any of your spiritual heritage. It need be of no concern to you if a group threatens you with such condemnation. God does not do it, neither can anyone else. For those that do must be the consequences of being judged as they judge.

27. DIVINE POWER IS AVAILABLE TO ALL

There is no divine power that is not directly available to you, as you are ready for it. No one and no organization has or has had any special dispensation. No one who truly has attained to spiritual awareness and consequent use of such power ever has claimed special privilege. This includes the Christed Jesus. Only those who do not understand such spiritual people and things claim this to be so, and they do so through lack of understanding to know or to use this power also.

Such privileges never are granted to favorites; God has no favorites. Those with spiritual understanding can and do perform higher works; they tell others that all could do the same. Those who lack spiritual understanding do not know how to do, and thus do not perform, higher works; they tell others they cannot do them either. "Choose this day whom you will follow."

28. RELIGIONS AND PHILOSOPHIES ARE PATHS, NOT GOALS

Religions and philosophies are of varying degrees of value to man when they truly seek to guide him on his spiritual quest. But even the best are only paths, not goals in themselves. Both should seek to carry mankind to the goal so the paths no longer will be necessary. This will be done best by placing man above and not below religion and philosophy. They are to serve man in his journey, not man to serve them for their inanimate perpetuation. The relationship of man to God, not man to a system, is the important concern.

29. CHURCHES ARE FOR MAN

Churches and similar organizations are of much value as such, so long as man has need of them. They are worthy of support in proportion to their real value. No statement in this book should be taken as argument against the existence of churches, but rather only against those practices which hinder man from learning the truth that would set him free.

30. THE MEANING OF CHURCH

Each person is a church unto himself or herself. This church, as meant by scriptures, is one's own congregation of spiritual thoughts.

31. EQUALITY OF ALL

No one in reality is favored in any way over any other. Race, color, sex, nationality, ancestry, work, actions or any other thing cannot change the basic spiritual equality of each and every person. Divine love knows and treats each one the same. It is errant human love, or lack of love, that judges falsely. It is important that each one so judging stop it, for not only does it add to error race thought but it also prevents one from receiving full divine love. This love ever is poured out in full to all. The amount one receives depends on how much he allows himself to receive. Again, as he judges so is he judged; he denies to himself whatever he denies to others. This may not be immediately apparent, but the law of cause and effect is not limited to man's concepts of time and space. Also, one cannot give out what he does not have.

32. TALENTS

Particular talents are not special divine favors. Everyone could not express in the same way in this period of life. Each one has some particular work he can do, if he will seek it and will do it.

33. YOU ARE IMPORTANT

You are important. There is a reason for your existence or you would not exist. You are the most important person in your world. You are the center around which your world revolves. Everyone is important; there are no unimportant people. But this is primarily true of your spiritual Self, not necessarily of your personal self. Learn of this true importance and be not misled by any sense of false importance.

34. NOT EVERYONE LIVES UP TO HIS REAL IMPORTANCE

No one is either more or less important than anyone else in eternal spiritual nature. But one may live up to this in varying degrees in his relative importance in this world.

35. GOD IS ALWAYS WITH MAN

Man is one with God whether he knows or believes it or not. Man is never separated from God, for God is man's very life. It is never necessary to search for God; you are always in His consciousness.

36. SEEING GOD

God is not a being with one physical form. God is all there is. Therefore, all forms whatsoever are forms of God. Wherever you look, you see God.

37. ALL IS DIVINE MIND

God is Mind, Spirit. All that exists is in Divine Mind. Mind is the medium of thoughts, the force that manifests thoughts, and the substance that composes, maintains and activates the manifestations.

38. NOTHING EXISTS BUT DIVINE MIND

Nothing exists outside Divine Mind, for God is infinite.

39. DIVINE MIND IS LIMITLESS

There is no limit to Divine Mind. Limits are man's ordinary concepts of time and space. There never could be any limit to time and space, even in the physical sense. Should there be any boundary beyond which there seemingly were no physical manifestations, it merely would mean nothing had manifested as yet known to man. Mind is there.

40. UNDERSTANDING INFINITY OF TIME AND SPACE

Time and space are limitless in Mind. Here is an experiment which will give you some idea what this means; further meditation along this line can give you a glimpse of the eternal nature of Mind and thus certain knowledge of your own eternal life. In a quiet place close your eyes. Make a mental concept of time. Think of as vast a past period as possible, then as far in the future as you can. No matter how far you imagine either way, mentally you still could add to it.

Now make a mental notation of the physical universes, just the idea of vast universes. Make it so vast an idea that it seems to take up all the space in your consciousness. Now mentally try adding more and more universes. There always would be room in mind for more, since you are making them only of mind. That is the way God creates them; the creations are made of Mind.

Even the initial trial of this experiment should give you an insight into the infinity of Mind, where there is no end of time or space. This is what is meant by no time and space in the spiritual realm:

not really neither time nor space but no concept of an end of time or manifestation. The concept of time and space is in terms of the duration and location of experiences, not of the end of everything.

41. YOUR ETERNAL NATURE

You are eternal. You never will cease to exist somewhere. It does no good to be afraid of ceasing, or hoping to cease, to exist. You will progress ever upward until eventually you unfold your real Self. Do not try to avoid it or to put it off, for you cannot do so indefinitely. When you do manifest your Self, then truly does your real life begin.

42. MAN IS ONE WITH DIVINE MIND

Man, as one with God, is one with all creation. The same Divine Mind that is man's body is also everyone and everything else. Thus man is one in what is called physical substance. The same Mind that moves all things also works at man's direction. Thus man is one in use of power. The same Mind by which God thinks is the Mind in and by which man thinks. This is why you do not see any references in this book to man's mind but only to man's consciousness or awareness. Man has no separate mind; he has consciousness in and use of the only Mind.

43. WHY MAN MUST LOVE ALL CREATION

Man must love all creations as part of God, and therefore as part of man's own Self. No man can love God and hate any of God's creations, for all such creations are part of God. For this reason man cannot convince Spirit he is expressing love, and thus deserves full spiritual recognition and use of spiritual powers, if he does not love everything. Remember that divine love for a person does not mean necessarily liking what he is doing. Thus it is possible to express divine love for one and still not like his temporary personality or actions. But love you must.

94

44. EFFECT OF LOVING ALL

You can help even those you never know by holding a constant feeling of love for all mankind. This helps greatly to destroy race thoughts of hatred and mistrust and to strengthen race thoughts of love.

45. DIVINE LOVE HOLDS NOTHING AGAINST ANYONE

When you have divine love, you do not, you cannot, hold anything against anyone else. It may seem difficult to forgive the wrongs of others, but it can and must be done. The experience of divine love is worth the effort. Even if no other benefits would appear to result, they most certainly will.

46. PRACTICING DIVINE LOVE

One should not wait for others to extend divine love to him before he extends it to them. He should begin immediately to practice love.

47. MAN EXPRESSES, NOT CREATES, LOVE

Man does not have to create love. It always exists everywhere, including within man. Man only need desire to let it express through him. This divine love will radiate through you to others if you allow it to flow to and through you. To do so, merely ask.

48. EXPRESSING GOD'S ATTRIBUTES

Man can express each of God's attributes in this same manner of asking to be a center for such expression.

49. GOD'S ATTRIBUTES ARE ALWAYS WITHIN MAN

All of God's attributes are latent within man; he need not search elsewhere. It is not necessary for man to attempt to define or to create these attributes; all he need do is call them forth. This applies to all divine attributes, including: love, peace, joy, health, understanding, harmony, strength, faith and imagination.

50. THE PERFECT PATTERN FOR MAN

Man has been created according to a perfect general pattern. This perfect image already is within everyone. Spiritual unfoldment consists of recognizing and manifesting the general pattern as a distinct individual. The general but complete pattern for spiritual man is Christhood. The term refers to any man or woman who completes spiritual unfoldment; it does not mean just one person only.

51. THE REAL TEACHING OF CHRIST JESUS

The teaching and works of Christ Jesus concern the attainment of each individual to the Christ status. Jesus did not in any way speak of himself as different from other men, except in degree of manifesting the Self. He repeatedly said he was not basically different and that all others could achieve the status he has.

52. GOD INCARNATE

Christ Jesus truly may be said to be God incarnate. So is every other person; there is no choice by man. But the degree of expressing God incarnated in each is a matter of individual choice.

53. SPIRITUAL MAN IS NOT ALOOF

No one who has attained spiritual awareness ever could desire to be set apart from others. Rather does he desire that others achieve and join in the more abundant life.

54. SPIRITUAL WORSHIP

The spiritually aware do not eliminate worship and praise of God. Their praise and thanksgiving are of a simple but understanding nature. Part of this worship is the recognizing and loving of all creations as God in manifestation. One must come to know, to love and to appreciate these manifestations, not only on the Earth but also in the planes which surround the Earth and in all dimensions throughout God's universes.

The spiritually aware have no part with pretentious show in the worship of God. It is unfortunate that some of those who profess to instruct others in the teachings of Jesus and other great spiritual leaders themselves indulge in the same pretentious adornment that Jesus denounced. They also heap the burdens on their followers that Jesus condemned. Nor is God in any way impressed with man's excessive or merely ritualistic fastings or ostentatious worship. Adequate mention of this is made in such scriptures as the Hebrew and Christian Bibles.

55. YOUR SEVEN BODIES

Although all do not resemble your physical body in form or appearance, each of your seven bodies of Earth life concern is an integral part of your total consciousness. Each vibrates at a different rate and each has the capacity to function in a different realm. You must reach the point of integration wherein each of your seven bodies is in perfect alignment, in order and in harmony and balance with the others. These bodies are: physical, mental, astral, emotional, etheric, and God consciousness, with the seventh not to be disclosed yet. There are other bodies, but you need not know of them at this time.

56. GOD KNOWS MAN'S THOUGHTS

True worship is in man's thoughts about God. Since God knows all man's thoughts, and since thoughts precede action, the physical acts of worship are not necessary. The reverse is not true: since God knows man's thoughts, his contrary actions cannot conceal the adverse thoughts that are behind the actions. "Be not deceived: God is not mocked."

57. THE SPIRITUAL HIERARCHY

There exists a spiritual Hierarchy for this planet and solar system, as for all others, which constitutes the spiritual government. The elohim, archangels, chohans, ascended masters and other agents of Spirit in many realms are entrusted with the creation, functioning, government, education and progress of this entire solar system and all creations within it, including man. The spiritual Hierarchy is the intermediary between God and the other kingdoms expressing on the planets and planes of this solar system. The spiritual ruler of Earth is Sananda, last incarnated on Earth as Christ Jesus. Each planet has such a ruler. Much additional information concerning the spiritual Hierarchy and its functions is available through Mark-Age.

58. YOU ARE NEVER ALONE

You never have been and never will be alone in your life expression anywhere, eternally. Your Christ Self is always present. With you at all times are one or more masters, teachers or guides of other realms. Their purpose in so being with you is to assist your spiritual understanding and progress in all ways possible under the divine law of free will. These teachers work with you under the direction of your own Christ Self, assisting in many ways. Many men on Earth are aware of these companions; all must become aware.

There are also beings of the human or other kingdoms on other planes and planets, all having life experiences. These include the elementals, devas, discarnates in the astral realms, Christ or etheric beings, celestials and others. The other realms of influence for a planet are the astral and the etheric. The astral is the abode of those who are between physical incarnations. Each planet has its own astral planes, not connected with or accessible by astrals to those of any other planet. The etheric planes are the abode of those who have progressed into the Christ realms and who are beyond need for further physical incarnation, although they often do so on missions. The etheric realms are continuous in the solar system, not separated for each planet as are the astral.

59. THE MARK AGE PERIOD OF TIME

This term is synonymous with the harvest period or the Latter Days and refers to the ending of the Piscean Age and the beginning of the Aquarian Age. A transition period lasting a spiritually symbolic forty years (1960–2000), Mark Age is the time promised when there will be signs in the sky or marks of the age to alert man on Earth that he is indeed in those times when there will be the ending of an age, but not of the physical world. It is the period of cleansing of all on Earth, including man, preparatory and prior to the Second Coming of Sananda as Christ Jesus of Nazareth. All is being raised to a higher vibration, mentally and physically as well as spiritually, for the Golden Age upon the Earth. This is to manifest beginning by approximately the year 2000. Many beings from throughout the universe are here to assist the Earth and all on it. The Mark-Age organization offers extensive information concerning this period.

60. THERE IS NO DEATH

All creations are life. There is no such state as death. All substance is God and therefore is life. There are various manifestations of life, with or without associated degrees of individual consciousness. What man mistakenly calls death is the end of one involved action of a manifested creation.

Thus a plant that is said to be dead still is composed of life, but the action has ceased on this plane which characterized its functioning in what usually is called life. In the so-called death of an animal or human body, the same is true. The body still is composed of life, but its activity of functioning as a body has diminished. Also, the consciousness that gave the body individual awareness and action no longer is associated with that body.

The body may change or even cease to manifest, but the life that composed it still exists, sooner or later becoming free to enter into other creation. This flow of atoms and molecules long has been known scientifically. Atoms are energy, which is life. The consciousness merely has severed its association. It has not ceased to live, for it is part of God's consciousness.

61. CONTROL BY THOUGHT

Man has the inherent spiritual power to control far more of the lower manifestations of life than most have imagined. He already has done this in many respects in what are termed physical and mental ways. He can do far more by thought, including control of what he believes to be inanimate objects and forces.

62. NOT MIND OVER MATTER

There is no such thing as mind over matter. This is not because matter cannot be controlled by mind, but because all is Mind. So-called matter actually is Mind or intelligent life acting in such manner as to produce manifestation. What is termed man's mind really is his consciousness in Mind, and thus his ability to direct the manifestation of intelligent life.

Therefore, what is called mind over matter, which denotes action of an animate force on a separate inanimate object, is in reality the direction of Mind by a consciousness in Mind to produce a certain result; which Mind does by becoming or acting as directed. Thus it is a case of harmonious working of Mind within, by and on Itself, not one of control of something else by a separate entity. This is worth much meditation and study, for it is the only method of creation and its control. Man's ideas of creation are limited understandings and uses of this only method.

63. THE KEY TO SPIRITUAL POWER

The key that unlocks spiritual understanding is the practice of divine love. Divine love must be inherent in the use of spiritual powers.

64. LOVE GOD AND LOVE ONE ANOTHER

These are the two main requirements for man in order to remain on Earth for the Golden Era. For only those who have achieved the Christ awakening can live here in the New Age, now dawning. Christ awakening means becoming aware of these two laws and seeking to express them fully; also recognizing and desiring Christ principles exclusively for one's own living. This awakening is a necessary step toward entering Christ consciousness, with its greatly increased permission and abilities to manifest spiritual talents and powers.

65. INFLUENCE BY THOUGHT

Spiritual powers include direct influence by thought on such as plant, animal and human life and on weather. Influence on man does not include violation of another's free will, except where use of free will intends harm to someone.

66. THOUGHT CONTROL OF WEATHER

Man long has been able to control weather by thought alone, both locally and in large areas. This covers every type of weather phenomenon. Such understanding is not at the disposal of any who are not aware of the possible effects of such control. Neither is weather control available in any way to those who would wish to use it against others, since "God sends His rain to fall on the just and the unjust alike."

67. VALUE OF ATTENTION
TO SPIRITUAL GUIDANCE

When governments, managed by men and women who are aware of man's spiritual nature and powers, seek the services of those with spiritual understanding and place proper facilities at their disposal, the developments will be almost unbelievably wondrous for all mankind. Such nations will have no further need to waste time, resources and money for protection from others.

Weather no longer will be disastrous and costly. New products will pour forth. New industries and labor harmony will solve economic problems. Peace and love will abound everywhere. Heaven will manifest on Earth. All of this depends on where man and his government and organizations focus attention. Such works now are sponsored by private individuals, but much more will be done as organizations, businesses, industries and governments provide the attention and the material resources needed and then utilize the results. Man must seek to foster spiritual works which would help rather than those others which would destroy him.

68. THE SOURCE OF REAL IDEAS

Divine Mind is the only source of real ideas. These ideas always are ready for man when he is able to receive them and to put them into use.

69. THE REAL PROTECTION AGAINST HARM

Man need not be subject to accidents. When he understands all is part of One and all is love and law, and uses common sense, nothing harmful can befall him. One also can extend this protection to others to a great extent.

70. PERFECT HEALTH

Man's heritage is perfect health. Man has the power to eliminate anything less than perfect health, for both himself and others. He is prevented from doing so only by his not knowing this, by his lack of belief, or by insufficient understanding and too little faith.

71. MAN'S PERFECT BODY

Man's inherent spiritual pattern for his body is perfect. It is not necessary to gain physical perfection or health; it is always within one's own consciousness. It is only necessary to call it forth and to accept it. The difficulty lies in personal and race thoughts that do not know and do not accept it. This also is true of mental health. The apparent hopelessness of any case does not alter this. The individual beliefs and, to a varying extent, the race thoughts pertaining to such cases are the only limiting factors.

However, man's health and body condition in this life may be controlled by his karma or special mission so that the visualized perfection will not manifest now, but in the next life. But still it is important to work for perfection now.

72. SPIRITUAL MAN UNAFFECTED BY WORLD AFFAIRS

One's real Self, the spiritual man, is not affected primarily by physical and mental acts or conditions. Spiritual man dwells eternally in peace, harmony, love and happiness. As one learns to live in his spiritual nature, he becomes less affected by worldly affairs, for he knows they are only experiences in his eternal life and not events in an only life. Therefore, he acts according to the scriptural advice: "Be in this world but not of this world." No matter how impossible or intolerable the situation, he is able to view it from his spiritual home, see it as unable to affect his spiritual being, and have it solved, all with perfect poise and detachment.

73. YOU ATTRACT ACCORDING TO YOUR THINKING

The law of attraction in the mental realm works in this manner: like attracts like. What one really wants he attracts to him: friends, abundance, health, opportunities, happiness, understanding and so forth; or the opposites. The determining factors are how one thinks and the feeling behind it. If one believes he gets only the negative, in reality he is asking for the negative. One can set his thoughts to any positive or negative degree and reap experiences accordingly. "As you sow, so shall you reap."

74. MIRACLES ARE IMPOSSIBLE

A miracle is an impossibility. What mistakenly are termed miracles are works which utilize either higher concepts of known laws or laws unknown to the observer. Divine law cannot be set aside by anyone; hence, miracles are not possible.

75. SPIRITUAL, MENTAL AND PHYSICAL REALMS ARE ONE

We speak of the spiritual, mental and physical as three realms. They really are one to those who understand all is spiritual and who act accordingly.

76. THE HOLY TRINITY

The Trinity is the Father, Son and Spirit. The main confusion concerning this concept has been the attempt to reconcile three entities with the idea of one God. Christian theology has confused additionally by trying to consider Jesus as the only son. Yet the concept is a simple one to understand when religious dogma has been cleared away. You have seen the Trinity explained several times in this book. There is only God, Divine Mind.

To understand creation, we regard this one Divine Mind as acting in three ways or phases. Father designates the phase which knows and thinks. It is the phase which activates creation by thinking ideas to be created, and so instructing. Son designates an idea of creation. Whether or not it be manifested already according to the image is not the criterion of creation, for it is in reality created once the Father so decides; the manifesting necessarily follows. Spirit designates the phase of action which manifests the creation. This is effected by Itself becoming and functioning as the manifestation.

The brief explanation: the one Mind creates by ideating, and Itself manifesting as, the creation. Thus God, Divine Mind, is one; which seems to function as three phases: Father, Son and Spirit.

Jesus rightfully may be considered as a son, since he manifested the divine idea of the species of man. But he is not the only son, for *Son* means a spiritual idea. Every man and woman becomes a son as he or she expresses the divine idea. *Son* is a term designating a general pattern of characteristics. An individual is one distinct manifestation which has the general characteristics contained in the idea, but also personal characteristics.

The analogy in brief, retaining the Trinity designations, is: Father, thinker; Son, idea; and Spirit, manifesting agent.

77. THE TRINITY OF MAN

Man, made in the image and likeness of God, also is a trinity. God is the infinite Trinity, man is the finite trinity. The only change is that man acts as the thinker, or creator; the remainder of this trinity is identical to the Holy Trinity.

78. FINITE AND INFINITE MAN

Man is both finite and infinite. As a finite incarnation of the infinite, he is able to think and to act in both ways.

79. OMNIPRESENCE, OMNISCIENCE AND OMNIPOTENCE OF MAN

Man is also omnipresent, omniscient and omnipotent. This is how spiritual works are initiated: in one's own consciousness.

80. MALE AND FEMALE

"And God created them, male and female created He them." This is true of man as a species, of the individual physical man or woman, and of the individual mental man or woman. The first is known to all. The second is accepted scientifically in that an individual has both male and female properties, the majority causing the sex of the physical body. There is relatively little difference physically, regardless of appearances. Your physical manifestation as male or female in no way determines your spiritual nature.

As for the mental, it depends in which way you are thinking. When you think of yourself basically as a physical being, your mental characteristics predominantly correspond to the sex of your body. But not exclusively, for otherwise there would be two complete ways of thinking about everything. When you think other than in terms of yourself as male or female, you are not thinking as either. If you expand this type of reasoning, you discover you often leave your physical self out of your thoughts. Thus the mental you functions in two manners, either as male or female or as neither.

This designation of male and female has been carried into many aspects of man's world, all of which convey the inner meaning. The male goes into the female to make one. Or, the male gives and the female receives to produce something. The seed, male, goes into the earth, female, to produce a plant. The analogy is always the same; it is a divine symbolization of the process of creation.

It applies to man in two basic and important spiritual functions: receiving and giving divine ideas. In the female or receiving capacity, one obtains ideas from Divine Mind. In the male or giving capacity, one implants ideas for Spirit to manifest. This is the inner meaning of the scripture that opens this particular discussion.

81. MEANING OF BOOK OF REVELATION

In the Christian Bible's Book of Revelation, or Apocalypse, the prophecies do not refer to literal events that are to take place in the outer world. They are analogous descriptions of one's inner overcoming as he begins the mental and spiritual process of eliminating error ideas. One who knows this finds the inner meanings of great value as he goes through the cleansing process, especially since he knows the process will be completed successfully and he glimpses the goal he will attain.

One who reads Revelation in the outer sense sees only fear and confusion. One who reads it understandingly sees wonderful and harmonious workings that lead to attainment of conscious at-onement with God. As with other scriptural writings which man is said to be incapable of understanding, attempts to interpret literally rather than spiritually, or physically rather than metaphysically, cause the failures to learn the lessons taught. It further leads to negative fears and hopelessness rather than to positive aids for attainment.

82. REAL MESSAGES OF HOLY BIBLES

In the outer reading, Bibles seem to deal with people and events of history which reveal divine laws and messages to man. To a large extent, but not always, this may be so. But in the inner spiritual reading, all people and events are symbolic instructions which reveal the proper steps and helps for attaining spiritual perfection. The Bibles of various religions are in reality spiritual textbooks when read under-standingly.

The Christian Bible is the most complete of such textbooks in that it tells of Christ Jesus, who not only achieved spiritual perfection on Earth but also gave invaluable specific instructions for similar attainment by others. These advanced instructions are contained in the inner meanings of both his words and acts. His acts served a double purpose: to instruct and to prove the instructions. In essence, both the Old and New Testaments are two books in one, an outer and an inner. The inner speaks not of other people but tells of your real Self and how to manifest this Self.

83. INSPIRED WRITINGS TEACH MAN'S TRUE NATURE

Bibles are only few of many inspired writings concerning man's real nature: his oneness with God. Great works in the Bibles are only a few examples of what man has achieved through the ages and of what increasing numbers of men and women are accomplishing daily now. "The works that I do, shall he do also; and greater works than these shall he do, because I go unto my Father." You too can go to your Father, who will give you great works to accomplish and will help you to accomplish them.

84. BUILDING A PERFECT BODY

One of the greatest works you can accomplish is the building of a body through which your real Self can express with no physical and mental limitations. Mental limitations are error ideas and thinking. Physical limitations include susceptibility to accidents and to weather conditions as well as to such conditions as sickness, dis-ease and impairments. For details, ask the architect and builder within. You will be taught.

85. ELIMINATION OF TRANSITION CALLED DEATH

One of man's most serious errors is anticipation of the transition he calls death. This transition has been established so firmly in race and individual thoughts as a necessary event that most people believe it to be eternally inevitable. It is not.

Some of the major causes of transition are: fully accepting it as inevitable; no desire to continue this particular life; stagnation due to refusal to learn or to do further constructive work; inability to let go of the past so as to change ideas and actions which prevent further learning and progress; not being or becoming a suitable expresser of abundant life; improper use of life in regard to self and others; failure to think in terms beyond the personal self; imperfect understanding; and insufficient thinking about prevention of the event.

But all can and will learn, at some time in their eternal experiences, "And there shall be no more death." This will occur for each when he learns how to resurrect the physical body, transmuting it so he can manifest it at any time there is need to use it on this or a similar plane.

86. LIVING NOW

Do not be concerned too much about the future. Make plans for your future in this life, but do not fail to see you also must live now. Do not concern yourself with what will happen to you after transition. You will learn of that when you are ready to learn, one way or another; by learning without having to make, or prior to making, the transition or after you have made it. Live now, in the eternal present. Now is eternity. No matter where or when you are in eternity, you have only now. Learn and do now; do not wait for some future place or time.

87. YOUR ONLY REAL POSSESSION

The only real thing you have is your consciousness. No matter how much material wealth you have, it is really only yours to use for a temporary period. All belongs to, since all is made of, Divine

Mind. You are not able to take material wealth with you in your next experience in your eternal journey. But it is important how you use it while you have custody.

Neither can you continue all of the pleasures made possible by the use of this world's material things. Many of them, yes, so it does behoove one to learn which are eternal and which are temporal. There are some temporal pleasures that are not only harmful but which hinder, halt or even set back your progress. These should be curbed or eliminated, as the case warrants. There are some temporal pleasures that are not only beneficial but which help one's progress, so long as they are not established so firmly they cannot be given up easily if not available later.

Since your consciousness or awareness is all you retain in your eternal experiences, it is vitally important that you develop your consciousness to that of your spiritual oneness, the expanding of your personal self until you are completely your real Self. All of the necessary information is available to you now on Earth. You can achieve your spiritual inheritance here and now.

88. REAL MEANING OF CRUCIFIXION AND RESURRECTION

One of the greatest instructive acts of Christ Jesus was the cruci-fixion–resurrection lesson. This was enacted to show man he must give up his personal self's limited viewpoint of life so he can rise to the manifestation of his real Self's limitless viewpoint. The act showed this expansion to the real Self does not mean elimination of the per-sonal identity or consciousness but rather a far greater expression of the personality; Jesus expressed as Jesus after the resurrection, and he still does.

He did not need to go through this for himself, but he did materi-ally prove the lesson. His act obviously did not accomplish this rising to Selfhood for anyone else; one must achieve for himself. But this act, recorded in race thought, when understood by anyone will reveal this inner meaning of what must be done and will make it easier to attain where Jesus did: in this life experience on this Earth. "I, if I am lifted up, will draw all men unto me." The more who achieve this same lifting up and demonstrate it to their fellowmen, the easier and sooner all will follow.

89. THE ONLY PARENT

"Call no man on earth your Father, for only one is your Father, even He who is in heaven." Families are sources of wonderful human relationships and experiences. However, you are really a spiritual being. Although this now includes your physical and mental identity on Earth, the real you derives ancestry from Spirit. Your physical and mental characteristics include all divine traits. One who takes pride in human ancestry does so falsely. One who sees all as equal parts of eternal oneness does so truly. In reality all have but one original ancestor: parent Mind.

90. MAN DOES NOT INHERIT IMPERFECTIONS

Man inherits bodily nothing physical or mental from his human ancestors directly; he inherits only tendencies. Spirit creates and develops the body according to the divinely ordained general human pattern, influenced by such factors as race, group and family. It is especially important that man know he does not inherit from others such error conditions as physical and mental imperfections and dis-ease.

He can receive and retain the belief that he has inherited a condition, even though he is not aware of it consciously. Therefore, it is necessary to impress the truth of impossible inheritance upon his consciousness so as to prevent the possibility of an inherited-error mental tendency concept from eventually manifesting in his physical or mental makeup. Since the inheritance only could be a mental tendency, it can be eliminated by mental action. Of course, man does inherit or carry over his own karmic reapings from previous lives.

91. THE PURPOSE OF PARENTHOOD

Proper initial understanding and directive planning by one, or preferably both, of the parents-to-be will help greatly in the manifestation of a child with perfect body and advanced mentality. Continued spiritual training by the parents will enable the child to come into spiritual awareness at an early age. This is the ultimate, and even now practiced, purpose of parenthood. Many highly evolved children are now incarnating, so special understandings and obligations are required of their parents.

92. PROPER PARENTAL TRAINING OF CHILDREN

The instillation in children of such error ideas as sickness, susceptibility to sickness, improper cautioning about sickness, fear of any kind, and death are deadly mistakes. Such actions may be motivated lovingly and protectingly, but they are based on misunderstandings of extremely serious degree. The proper policy is to extend divine protection, while withholding error ideas, until proper spiritual instruction can be initiated.

Much of one's basic error thought pattern is impressed upon him in his early childhood and remains a strong influence on his adult thinking, even though he apparently long ago may have forgotten it. This is a serious responsibility of parenthood. A child is not in reality the parents' possession but is an independent spiritual being who is manifesting in another role as an expresser of God.

The parents are to help in the unfoldment of the child's consciousness as much as they are able. This carries with it the Self-contained and Self-given reward of increased spiritual awareness and gifts for the parents. Actually, the training can begin within each parent long before parenthood, in the consciousness of man and wife.

93. BE INTERESTED IN ALL CREATION

Take time to take interest in all creation as does a child. Each creation is the manifestation of a divine idea. Proper attention can reveal a lesson in spiritual understanding.

94. YOUR MOST IMPORTANT ACTION

Take a lesson from childhood days. The most important thing is what you are doing and the most important place is where you are doing it. Of course, unlike the child, you have other considerations, but it is important that you do well what you are doing at any particular time. For even though you may be doing several things at that time, it is all you are doing then.

95. YOU ARE AGELESS

The spiritual you has no age. As you understand this you will stop regarding yourself in terms of physical and mental age. It is never too early or too late to acquire spiritual understanding and to put it to use. Physical age is an excuse, not a reason, for failure to learn.

96. POSITIVE THINKING FOR GREATER USE OF TIME

One who eliminates error ideas and fears from his consciousness, and it can be done completely, discovers he has more time at his disposal than he ever dreamed possible. This is due in large part to the better utilization of time formerly spent in entertaining such negative thoughts as fears, worries, condemnations, misgivings, hate, mistrust, sickness, accidents, death, insecurity, inharmony, unrest, old age and many others. Also there are the wandering thoughts such as concern the nature and purpose of life. One with spiritual understanding has eliminated all negative thoughts and knows or is learning the nature of life.

If you as yet have not eliminated negative thoughts from your consciousness, make an analysis yourself and see just how much of your time, both awake and asleep, is spent with or influenced by such thoughts. Mark this time as unproductive to spiritual progress and work. Then try to visualize what even a small part of that time spent in positive productive thought could accomplish. Unfortunately for analysis purposes, you barely could begin to imagine the results, but what you could imagine should be enough to convince you of the time and benefits you would gain.

97. MAN CANNOT DISRUPT UNIVERSAL HARMONY

Man cannot upset the harmony of the universe. He cannot destroy mankind or Earth. He cannot carry negative thoughts and actions away from Earth. There is no need for concern that such could happen; it is impossible.

98. FREEING THOSE WHO HAVE PASSED ON

The transition called death is not the end of an individual's existence. It is the closing of one experience before beginning another. No one remaining here has any claim on one who has passed on; each is a free spiritual being. Naturally, one who passed on usually will be missed, especially by those of close association. But much of such grief is selfish; not thoughts of the welfare of the one who has gone on but of the effect on those who stayed. Loose such a one and let him go, for the benefit of all concerned.

Life still wishes to express here as and through those who still are here. Graves are no place for attention. The bodies placed there are of no further value to those who used them, so they no longer are associated with those bodies. It is much better remembrance to regard them as living, which they are, than as in graves, where they are not. The only death in a cemetery is in the consciousness of those who visit it. Seek not the living there; they are doing their living elsewhere now. There is no death except in man's limited belief in it. Life is eternal. It changes in manifested forms but it never ends.

99. PERSONAL WORSHIP AND SUPERSTITION HAVE NO PLACE IN THE SPIRITUAL

Man should not worship anyone or anything except God in everyone and everything. Worship is used here in the religious sense. No spiritually aware person, however high his unfoldment, ever has asked for or has wanted personal worship; nor ever could do so. Such persons always seek to show God as equally one with all. Great works are done to manifest divinity and to prove each one's Godhood, not for personal glory.

As for worship of powers less than God, there are none. Any power is divine; any power other than divine cannot exist. This applies especially to all superstitions. There is no power whatsoever in any superstition, other than the power of established conscious and subconscious belief. Deny any further belief in all superstitions and be free from fears of unknown powers over you. Personal worship and superstition are not found in spiritual awareness.

100. A DIVINE DECREE

All is well. Thus it is eternally in the spiritual. This your spiritual Self knows. Whatever outer conditions may appear to be, your real Self always knows all is well. Let this judgment prevail. No matter what may happen, let this be your divine decree: all is well.

▲

III. 50 HOW-TO'S

These are examples of how to do, or how to have done, specific things. As you use one, phrase the idea in your own words. Remember that the actual wording is not the important thing; the idea and your emphatic feeling of the idea as applied to you are important. Some examples of how to phrase ideas are given, but only for illustration. When it is for yourself, think of your already being, having or doing it: *I am, I have* or *I am doing*; this is of great importance. When it is for someone else, in your own thinking see him, her or them as already being, having or doing it. When it is for some manifestation, action, event or other purpose, in your own consciousness see it as already completed.

Always remember your part of the process of doing all things is: (1) deciding what you want done, (2) directing that it be done, (3) establishing it in your own consciousness as already done, and (4) allowing it to be done, doing anything you may have to in order to help it come to pass but not directing how it must be done or otherwise interfering.

Although all is Spirit, at first you may find it easier to understand if you address your requests variously; but always remember that all of these are workings of Spirit. For those applying to yourself, you may regard statements as addressed to either your spiritual Self or subconscious. For others, think of their corresponding phases of consciousness. For all other things, think in terms of Spirit.

Before making your statement, be certain to examine it to see if it is in any way negative. Do not include, in the statement or in your thinking about it, what you do not want. Often this means deliberate refusal to recognize appearances. If it is not as you want it, see it as you want it and not as it is. Make certain your statement contains what you are requesting. It is not usually necessary to include specific details, but do be sure it concerns a specific desire. Do not have any doubts as to it being accomplished, your worthiness or any other misgivings.

In general, maintain a completely positive feeling which includes praise, belief in receiving, and thanks. Your thanksgiving consists of thanks for God and all true creation, for your own being, for the powers at your disposal, for your right to ask for what you want, and for the granting and receiving of the request.

These are relatively few examples here of how to do specific things. They are intended to give some idea as to the wide application of this principle of doing things by having them done for you. You will be able to think of many more ways to use the principle, generally and specifically, for yourself and others. Do not think you are being presumptuous or that you can make too great use of this idea; it is your right and your purpose. The greater and wiser use you make of this fundamental spiritual principle, the better you and all else will be. To avoid repetition, each of the following examples will not begin with *how to,* although in each case it is implied.

1. DO ALL THINGS

The master key to do all things is asking Spirit, the all-knowing Creator, to do it. It is well that this be the first how-to you learn and do. The subject has been covered adequately in the first section of this book. Here is an illustration of how to phrase a request: "I am one with Divine Mind. I now ask Spirit to guide my spiritual unfoldment. I give my permission for You to guide me in whatever ways You know are best. I am open and receptive to Your instruction through whatever sources You wish to use. No false instruction from any other source will have any effect on me. So be it. Thank You."

2. ACHIEVE PERSONAL UNITY

For early practical purposes of understanding and working, you may regard yourself as a trinity of three phases of consciousness. But remember this is only to avoid initial confusion which might result from trying to understand how your consciousness in reality is one and yet does things without your being aware of them. The three phases of your one consciousness may be regarded and addressed as superconscious, conscious and subconscious. This same trinity appears in the Christian Bible as Christ, husband or man, and wife or woman, in the same order as above.

Speaking as the conscious phase, ask that all three phases henceforth work together in divine order and harmony according to the divine plan of your being. Each phase is to perform its work to perfection. There will be no attempt to shirk responsibility or to assume any unauthorized control. The order of authority is superconscious or real Self, conscious, subconscious.

The Self is one with the source of wisdom, the knower of all things, the instructor and guide, Spirit. The conscious phase is the executive which makes decisions and initiates action. The subconscious is the phase which constantly re-creates the entire body, maintains it and all its functions, and performs your requests. It is able to do all these things and is at your command for proper use. All three phases should work together as a whole.

As you advance you will be able to understand that the conscious phase is your individual awareness within Divine Mind and that the other two phases are your individual use of the corresponding two phases of Divine Mind. Your conscious phase expands to become aware of knowledge now seemingly held by the other phases and not known yet to you consciously.

But it is fortunate that for now much of this is not known to you. If it were, you would devote too much time trying to manage them and too little time to increasing your ability to make decisions, which is part of your role as a creative expresser of God. So, see yourself as a perfect unity that knows how to perform each detail of the divine pattern with increasing understanding. Decree this perfect working now.

3. UNDERSTAND THE SCIENCE OF MIND

God does everything according to divine law. Every part of divine law, each specialized law of the general law, is an exact, eternal and never-varying principle. The science of man is based primarily on facts, and facts are changeable. The science of God is based on actualities, and these are not changeable. Divine Mind acts according to exact laws which eternally produce results that cannot vary. It is important that you know everything happens exactly according to these natural laws. In order to achieve a workable understanding of higher things, you must know that everything happens according to changeless laws.

This makes it necessary that you learn these laws so you can work with them and obtain predictable results rather than in ignorance of them and obtain no or varied results. It has been proved sufficiently by science that what has seemed impossible or what even had not been imagined is achieved through understanding of higher laws previously not known or comprehended. What seems impossible by one law is made possible not by breaking that law but by more fully understanding it or a higher law and working in obedience to it.

Establish in your thinking the existence of divine law, with a multitude of component natural laws, and your desire to learn and to follow these spiritual principles. "I am always in complete accord with divine law. I am one with divine order and harmony. I respectfully wish to understand spiritual laws so I may act obediently in such manner as to achieve according to my inherent spiritual nature. I ask divine guidance in this, knowing I will not be allowed to act contrary to any law which would harm me or others. So be it."

4. USE DIVINE SCIENCE

Put yourself in harmony with Divine Mind as explained in how-to #3. Understand that all things work according to divine law with such unfailing exactness that there could be no more perfect example of scientific principles. God is Omni-science. Outside of God there is no knowledge of anything; there is nothing but God. There is no science but divine science.

A further analysis of Omniscience reveals another interesting way of looking at science. Om-ni-science. Om is an ancient name for God and *ni* means *nothing*. Thus we have God-science or the science of God. Nothing is in between God and science. The world of science as a whole has come ever closer to proving that all manifestation is an exact scientific proof of the laws of infinite consciousness. Many scientists individually have known and have said so.

To use divine science you can proceed in one or both of two ways. One is to seek information about a specific law which will enable you to accomplish a particular thing. The other is to seek a general law, perhaps one yet unknown to man of Earth, which will open new fields. Of course, you apply this science in all your initiating action. Here is an illustration of a how-to for specific information: "I am now quiet. I cease my own thinking about the problem of how to achieve this result. I am now receptive to Spirit's solution."

Allow ample time for your meditation. The answer may come during that meditation or a subsequent one, it may seem just to occur to you, it may come through another source, or it might come through an apparently accidental happening. Or the answer might be nothing, indicating no answer. Man would save tremendous time and work now needlessly spent if only he would turn to Divine Mind in this way for the inspiration that continually is being offered.

Regarding simultaneous receiving of ideas by two or more persons, know that Divine Mind is the source of all true fundamental ideas and they are available to anyone who is qualified, regardless of man's opinions as to which person or nation should have them.

5. LEARN TRUTH

Express the earnest desire to Spirit that you want to learn and to use only truth. Ask that all error ideas be eliminated in the proper manner and time and that no error ideas henceforth be allowed to be impressed in your consciousness. Ask that you learn how to recognize truth; it will come gradually as an inner knowing, a feeling of truth. Request that you receive constantly more truth and state that you will use it.

"I now inform the subconscious that the superconscious will guide in elimination of all error ideas already established in consciousness. It has supreme authority, even above my conscious decrees, in this elimination and in the impression of all future ideas. It has the power to cancel any decrees that are not proper. I am receptive to ideas of truth. I am able to recognize truth."

6. MAINTAIN YOUR BODY PERFECTLY

There is a divine plan of the human body, both the male and the female. It is a general plan and allows for individual variances within specified limits. But it is a perfect plan; there are no imperfections included. Body imperfections and malfunctions are due to man's imperfect consciousness. They may be brought forth by the one affected or by others. They may be caused by thinking or doing something wrong, or by not thinking or not doing something that should be done; error of commission or omission. This perfect spiritual pattern is inherent in everyone. It is the function of forces of Spirit to manifest the body, which is why it continues manifestation after consciousness leaves it in the transition called death.

You may address your requests concerning the body directly to Spirit. This requires the higher recognition that Spirit manifests as your body; it produces the best results quicker. Or at first you may wish to think of it as addressing the subconscious; since it is really your use of Spirit, this is actually the same thing but it may seem more personal. Also it may take more time and more of your attention to produce results. This depends entirely on your own ability to understand the relationship, since it is your degree of belief that determines the result.

In your statement, request that your body be manifested and maintained according to the inherent spiritual pattern. Do not believe this will be done by requesting it only once. Devote some time to it daily or several times a week. Always see your body as already perfect in your thoughts.

"I have a perfect body. I am one with my perfect physical body, as it is imaged in Divine Mind. I now request Spirit (or subconscious) to manifest my body according to the inherent perfect pattern. Every part of my body manifests according to the divine plan. Every function of my body is always according to divine order and harmony. I do not attempt consciously to dictate how my body should function, for that is known and taken care of by Spirit acting through the subconscious. So be it. Thank You."

7. CORRECT BODY IMPERFECTIONS

This will refer mainly to the body as it now physically exists. It is possible to have parts that are missing and deemed irreplaceable once more manifested. This has been demonstrated, but it requires a high degree of understanding and faith. Parts that still exist physically but in imperfect condition are included in the following discussion. For every body part there is a perfect plan of its makeup and function in Divine Mind.

Why then are there imperfections? Because all things work according to natural laws, one of which is the law of cause and effect. When certain causes are initiated, knowingly or unknowingly, deliberately or unintentionally, or even just by the way things occur, corresponding effects result.

It is said nothing happens by chance, that man's thinking is the result of all that happens to him. This is only partially correct. Man is subject to chance, as are other manifested creations on Earth, when courses of action independent of him interact to produce other causes and effects. His thinking in itself may not produce it, but it still affects him. However, his thinking may allow it to affect him by his omission to have placed himself so in divine order and harmony with all things that he is under divine protection at all times. When one does invoke this protection, he is not subject to chance.

"I am one with divine love. All things in my experiences move in divine order and harmony; no accidents or harm can befall me. Spirit gives me divine protection at all times. I also ask this divine protection for those whom I know, and I place them in Spirit's care. I realize that by so asking I do not in any way interfere with their freedom of will and their right to learn in whatever way Spirit deems best. I know I must do my part, using common sense at all times."

Regardless of the cause of imperfection, the body still can be made perfect. Sometimes this can be done by physical correction, for this too is a divine method. In some cases this may be accomplished quickly in such a manner, but only because most have more belief and faith in that way. For in reality Spirit creates everything by becoming and functioning as everything. This is an impersonal manifesting, as though Spirit had no knowledge of what It was acting as

121

in any particular manifestation. Actually, the manifesting is done according to divine plans.

What man terms imperfections are really the effects of other actions on that manifestation, resulting in a change due to natural laws. But the original plan is still inherent in the creation. A return to perfect manifestation is asking Spirit to manifest that part according to its inherent and perfect divine pattern. One purpose of this book is to teach you how to know you are able to do this.

This applies to correcting imperfections in all other forms of what mistakenly is designated as animate life. For example, a tree, which does not have the degree of consciousness associated with it that an animal or man does, can be caused to manifest again according to the inherent spiritual plan of its manifestation after it has become what erroneously is called dead. Its apparent nonfunctioning is merely the cessation of its manifesting in the higher degree called life. Spirit still is manifesting in the lower degree as the physical form of the tree.

Man has the power to ask Spirit to manifest the tree once more according to the complete inherent pattern, providing it is done in time for compliance during the normal spring reawakening period, if it is of that type. One also can ask for perfect, and even special, growth of plants when planting and caring for them.

It is not necessary that you consciously know the details of the perfect pattern, or even of the imperfect condition. Neither is it necessary that you know how or where the inherent pattern is and how Spirit follows it; only that it exists in Divine Mind and that Spirit knows how to do all things.

It is well to mention a caution for those seeking to correct physical and mental imperfections, malfunctions and illness in this manner. It is not suggested that one who has not achieved this understanding yet, or who does not have the assistance of one who has, neglect other familiar methods when a condition is of a serious or critical nature.

Such other help does not lessen what here is termed the spiritual way, for God has methods corresponding to physical, mental and spiritual levels of understanding. Nothing can set aside the spiritual. The belief that physical and mental methods cannot be used limits those who believe so and often results in unneeded suffering and delay in correcting the error condition.

However, the spiritual method of directly invoking Spirit's action can effect the work in every case, dependent on the understanding behind the speaking of the word and any karmic condition. Even when it seems advisable to turn to additional methods, the decree method also should be used with as much faith as possible.

It is not necessary to attempt to speak the word for every part of the body. "I am one with Spirit. I ask that You manifest my entire body according to the inherent divine pattern of perfection. Every part of my body is and always will be perfect. Every function of my body now and always performs in divine order and harmony according to the inherent plan. I give thanks to You for this perfect body, which always permits me to manifest in this world with no physical impediments. So be it."

However, if a particular part or function requires individual attention, proceed as above, prefacing the treatment by mentioning the part or function but not its imperfect condition. When speaking the word for someone else, and this holds true regardless of the purpose, precede your statement with the name and at least general address of that person, plus a mental picture of that person if possible. This is to indicate clearly for whom the work is being done.

Finally, remember what you learned in the first section of this book: spiritual unfoldment and the subsequent increase in ability to initiate action by Spirit is a gradual process. Therefore, do not expect results at first by just once making a brief request. The examples given here should be considered only as guides upon which to make your own affirmations, decrees or other forms of requests. Depending upon the nature of the request, it should be held in your thoughts for at least several minutes, and as often as deemed necessary thereafter until the desired result has been produced.

But do not limit your eventual attainment by believing you always will have to make a decree, visualization or realization of long duration or more than once. When you have had sufficient experience in having your requests correctly manifested, begin to aim at the goal of just one or two sentences, or a brief thought, made once. It not only enables you to do more but it also frees you from further work and concern for the same case. This how-to is lengthy, detailed and of wide scope, but it is that way so as to give a view of the general field of all so-called animate life.

8. ELIMINATE DISEASE

Disease is an impersonal manifestation of Spirit. The organisms said to cause disease themselves are caused by something else and so are only secondary causes. Therefore, to eliminate disease completely, the initial cause must be eliminated or changed. The real cause of all manifestation is thought. God creates only perfection, with all things guided by love and therefore acting in perfect order and harmony. Man creates perfection and imperfection.

Since diseased areas do not exhibit perfect order and harmony, disease is a creation of man. Therefore, disease must be eliminated by eliminating error thoughts and wrong thinking. The organisms which physically cause disease are Spirit's impersonal manifestations of man's thoughts. This is of the utmost significance, for to understand it is not only to know how to eliminate disease but also to know how it is eliminated.

Mankind is solely responsible for disease. Why does an individual become affected? First of all, if he reaches the understanding that disease does not exist in the reality of the spiritual realm and if he then sets his thinking in order, he never will be affected by disease; unless it pertains to a specific role he is enacting.

As for those who are affected, there are several reasons due to improper thinking: The specific thoughts of the individual may cause the corresponding specific error manifestation in himself. His error thinking as a whole may make him liable for a certain class, or even just any, error condition of disease. A lack of error thinking but also the lack of not having declared himself immune can bring disease, since all are part of mass consciousness.

Children, since they are part of mankind too, are liable also to error conditions resulting from error race thoughts, unless someone specifically has exempted them by proper spiritual treatment (see #91 and #92 of the second section). As to animals and plant life: of all manifested creations on Earth, man alone by his thinking is able to affect other creations, and does so, both favorably and adversely. Speaking of causes, these also apply to how-to #7, concerning imperfections.

How to eliminate disease, with such a list of causes to consider? It may be necessary to discover and to correct the error thought, if held by the person affected, so the condition or another one will not reappear. But if the error thought is not serious or is no longer actively held, it is not generally necessary to search for it.

When the above is not the cause, or the error thought has been corrected, the treatment is simply requesting Spirit no longer to manifest the error condition. Or, in your own consciousness, no longer see the error condition manifested, whether the work is for you or another. It will be necessary also to ask Spirit to manifest according to the inherent perfect spiritual pattern when some part or function was altered materially. Children can be protected to a great extent from being affected by error thoughts until they have grown enough to be responsible for their own thinking.

How can it be said that Spirit manifests as these organisms? Because Spirit is the only manifesting power or substance there is. Then why manifest as evil creations? They are completely impersonal manifestations by Spirit and, like all manifestations, are neither good nor evil, they just are. Man's thoughts caused such manifestations.

This is the reason, regardless of physical medical research, that all disease never could be eliminated until mankind's error, disease-creating thoughts were eliminated. That is why new diseases always seemed to await medical research; one major disease seemed to be controlled only to have other major ones develop.

But what happens to the diseased material which has been eliminated? That depends partly on the degree of understanding of the one effecting the spiritual treatment. It may disappear gradually or it may disappear quickly, even instantaneously. In the former it may be eliminated by seemingly normal methods of the body. In the rapid and instantaneous elimination, it is because Spirit just ceases to manifest the error condition, thus freeing the energy from that manifestation. The eliminated material does not go anywhere; Spirit merely has ceased to be that form.

This does not, since it could not, violate any natural law. Material substance is in reality energy acting in such a manner that it seems to be matter. When the energy no longer acts to produce the manifestation, the manifestation ceases. This change from manifestation to nonmanifestation can be so rapid that to man, who is used to limited time concepts, it seems instantaneous. The reverse, seemingly instantaneous change by energy from nonmanifestation to manifestation, is also possible. How? Spirit is the manifesting agent.

Of course, it takes a high understanding and highly established ability of initiating Spirit's action to be able to do such things. It can be and has been done. All eventually will be able to do this; therefore, it is evident why each must learn how to create perfectly. It is by divine grace that man cannot have all his requests manifested until he learns to think properly.

"In my spiritual consciousness I now ask Spirit no longer to manifest that error condition but henceforth to manifest here according to the perfect spiritual pattern. I thank You that You already have granted this request. So be it. Thank You for this gift, also."

9. PREVENT SICKNESS

This is a matter of denial and affirmation. The denial phase may be regarded in two parts. One is the elimination of any ideas or ways of thinking that result in disharmony of the body. The other is the elimination of the error idea that you are able to be sick. Your inherent body-plan is perfect, which includes its functioning in order and harmony. God's plan of the human body does not include sickness or any other dis-order or dis-ease.

Neither does God ever cause such things. Man causes them by either thinking wrong or not thinking right, by mistakes of commission or of omission, or for certain spiritual demonstrations. Since you do not remember all the wrong ideas that have been impressed on your memory since infancy, let alone past lives, it would be a long and difficult task to attempt to find and to correct them. But you can have it done by asking Spirit to do it for you, and it will be done.

The affirmation phase consists in establishing in your consciousness the new decree that never again can you be sick. Of course, you must not return to thoughts and fears of sickness, and you must not indulge in any inharmonious or error thinking that would result in sickness. In brief, you must decree no more sickness and you must not violate that decree yourself.

It may not be easy for those who believe sickness is a real part of life, and especially those who have experienced much of it, to eliminate all belief in and fear of sickness, but persistent efforts to do so will be successful. There are many who consciously do not know this basic principle of no sickness in reality but who nevertheless do not experience illness. They just do not believe they will get sick and they are not afraid they will get sick, so they do not.

"I am one with perfect order and harmony. I constantly express the divine plan of perfect order and harmony in my thinking and body. I now deny further belief in any sickness. I ask Spirit to help in the elimination of all belief in sickness that may exist in my memory. I ask You to guide my thinking so no thoughts of mine or of others ever can manifest as sickness in my thinking and body.

"In spiritual consciousness I now know that never again will I experience sickness in my thinking or in my body. This is an order, which I now establish and which must be obeyed. So be it. Thank You for Your perfect plan and for having given to all of us the power to establish this plan by our agreeing to it and accepting it."

10. CONTROL YOUR WEIGHT

Maintaining proper body weight is easy and effortless when done mentally. There is no need for special diets or calorie counting. You can eat what you wish so long as eating is moderate and sensible. There is no need for special exercise.

All you need do is set the weight you want and instruct your body to manifest it or whatever weight is proper. Establish this as a firm decree, strengthen your belief that it will be so, do this for several days or weeks and then forget it. You soon will notice results and you will reach your proper weight, if you really have believed it possible and if your eating habits have been moderate.

"I see myself weighing (so many) pounds. I now establish this as the weight of my body and instruct my subconscious to manifest

127

accordingly. I give thanks that my body remains at approximately such weight. It is well done. So be it."

11. HAVE ABUNDANT PERSONAL ENERGY

Spirit is the only energy, regardless of how many forms and sources there seem to be. When man seeks energy by looking elsewhere than to Spirit, he still will find it but he will not do so as easily or use it as fully as when he recognizes and turns to Spirit directly. This is especially true with body energy, for Spirit is functioning already in a highly complex manner as your body.

When we think and act improperly, we misdirect the natural body energy into needless or excessive activities. Our excessive or continued misdirection interferes with the body's natural tendency to correct such mistakes. We further can complicate this corrective action by personal attempts to determine the manner in which it should be done. The body is composed entirely of intelligent life and needs only our cooperation, not direction by our limited conscious understanding.

The use of medicines, including vitamins, indeed may be of some value in restoring energy, but it can be an interference if it constitutes a limited directive as to how the energy must be obtained. Turn directly to Spirit, state that you wish to use body energy properly, and ask that you experience abundant energy.

"I am one with the only energy there is: Spirit. I do not have to add energy to my system for I am always one with all the energy there is. I have an unlimited supply of body energy and I use it wisely. Energy constantly fills every part of my body; it is my body. I thank You, dear Spirit, for You as energy, and I constantly manifest it abundantly. I do not limit the supply of energy by attempting to dictate how it must be supplied; You supply it directly by being it."

12. ENJOY MORE ABUNDANT LIFE

Regardless of how little or how much you now are experiencing or enjoying life, you joyfully can experience far more. Life has glorious experiences awaiting you that you cannot begin to imagine. No matter what your past or present experiences, life is able and is anxious to express more fully as and through you. You have only to desire it earnestly and not deny the possibility. For you to enjoy life you must allow life to express through, not on, you. God can express through you only as much as you permit. God does not give life, God is life. As you express God you express life.

Many have become disinterested in life because they think there can be no further happiness for them. This is never true. Nor need you wait for another life. You already have access to all the life you can use. Those who do not allow life to express ever more fully through them are limiting God. Those who do not care to live and those who have withdrawn from interest in expressing life in reality may be committing a form of suicide, for life will not maintain for long a useless channel of expression. This is the law of life: live! The purpose of life is living. Life must express eternally.

Open to life and you will find life opening to you. Ask that God express freely through you. It is well to ask for certain pleasures and things in life, but do not limit what you may experience. There are reasons for your being here or you would not be here. Those reasons include enjoyment of life, with pleasures you cannot imagine. So in your asking, permit your Self to do the final choosing, thus leaving the way open for greater good than you request. If you do not get that for which you ask, look for something better to come. Place complete guidance and faith in your Self to express life fully through you.

"I am one with life. My purpose is to express life. I now ask my Self to express fully through me as me. Spirit goes before and opens life to me. I am a center of ever-expanding abundant life that knows no limitations. I now open my understanding to receive the kingdom that has been prepared for me since the beginning. 'And now, O Father, glorify me with Your Own Self with the glory which I had with You before the world was.' So it is. Thank You."

13. BE FREE FROM FEARS

Those who know oneness with God have no fears of any kind. This may sound difficult to believe for those who still have fears. Yet, it is difficult for those who have eliminated fears to recall what it was like to have them. Not having fears and knowing why you never will have them are not necessarily the same. The latter denotes spiritual understanding that there is nothing to fear, that nothing can possibly harm you, because God is love. The former is seldom a complete freedom from fear and does not guarantee complete safety without a belief in the protection of divine love. "Perfect love casts out fear."

Place yourself in full accord with perfect love and you will recognize and will be recognized by love in all creation. There are no evil powers you need fear, and wrong use of power will not be able to work against you. There is no devil or other superstition to harm you. False belief in them causes it to seem they have power, but it is only the power which you give by believing in them. Take back that power by denying any further belief in them.

"I am one with perfect love. God is love. There is nothing real but God; and God is good. I know only good is real. Therefore, anything not good is not real and I have nothing in reality to fear. I take back all power I have given to any fear and superstition, including Satan. There is no fear in the spiritual realm, so I cast out all fears as I enter into my real home in Spirit.

"I ask, dear Spirit, that You eliminate any subconscious fears stored in my memory. I further ask that You make me consciously aware that I have absolutely nothing to fear, for You are all there is and You are love. So be it. I never again can be afraid of anything. Thank You, dear God."

14. HAVE HARMONIOUS AFFAIRS

God is. Besides God, nothing is. God is all. "I am one with You, dear God. Therefore, I am one with all that is; one with all creation, manifested or unmanifested. Everything functions according to divine order and harmony; nothing can exist in reality that is not in divine order and harmony. I always wish to think and to act in perfect accord with You.

"I ask that You guide my affairs at all times and permit me not to act in any but perfect ways, 'for You will not lead me into temptations but You will deliver me from evil, for Yours is the power.'

130

Spirit goes ahead in all my affairs and prepares the way so that all works in divine order and harmony. I radiate love and blessings to all persons and to all things, and wish order and harmony for them. All is well. Thank You, Father-Mother Mind, for all of this and more. So be it."

15. BE AT PEACE

Spirit knows only peace. This means that although God does know when we are not at peace, He also knows that such lack of peace is not real. This means there is only peace in the spiritual realm; man sees and acts otherwise. God also knows your spiritual being has constant and eternal rest. Our experiences on Earth are but temporary ones. They will pass and will be forgotten in our eternal living. Already you have forgotten countless experiences in this life, many of which were important at the time, and probably recall little or nothing from previous lives.

Within your total consciousness your Self sees all experiences in relation to your eternal life and evaluates them far better than you can with your limited conscious knowledge and vision. No matter how hopeless or desperate an experience seems, it is only temporary and cannot affect your real Self. The real you is always at complete peace. You can develop the ability to raise your thinking to the spiritual level from whence you view all things in eternal peace. From here you can examine the temporal experience and decide or learn how to handle it.

"I am one with eternal peace. I constantly know the peace that truly passes all understanding. When anything would seem to be less than peaceful, I have but to express Your peace. I do not need to seek that peace, for it is always part of me and I of it. I have but to imagine myself on another planet and the events on this one seem such a small part of Your eternal and infinite creation. Or I have but to imagine if I no longer were to express on Earth that all still would go on.

"I so fully and completely express Your peace that it constantly radiates through me to all who are in my thoughts and presence. In this way all are led to know and to express Your eternal peace. All is well. Thank You, dear God, for this gift which I use freely and radiate abundantly to all."

16. ELIMINATE WORRY

Worry has no place in reality. In the spiritual realm, only the realities are considered and situations never are judged by appearances. When you view things from your spiritual consciousness, you know all things must go well. If conditions seem to be going wrong, it is only because you cannot see all the aspects and possibilities. You have not used your spiritual understanding and power to correct it or you are doing something wrong.

You will have, and will come to welcome, problems of yours and others, but you never need worry about them. If you cannot handle or solve one, you know who can: Spirit. No matter how impossible a situation may seem to you, God already knows how to solve it and easily can do so. Nor is constant turning to God for help in any way wrong. "Let Him who is greatest among you serve you." This you fully understand when you learn that all help you ask for is Self-help. Part of your work is to help others with their problems and another part is to solve problems yourself, but solving problems never should cause worry. If it does you can be sure you are not acting in your full spiritual nature; partly, perhaps, but not fully.

"I am one with Spirit, who knows how to solve all problems. I know there never is any reason for me to worry about anything, for You know of every need I have. I face each problem knowing all is well and the problem already is solved in Your Mind, or else the problem really does not exist. If I cannot see the solution, I place it in Your care, knowing I then can forget it and only do what You direct. I now ask that if I ever should forget, and begin to worry, You immediately remind me all is well. I thank You, dear God, for the blessing of never again having any worries. So be it."

17. BE POISED

When you are vibrantly aware of your oneness with Spirit and thus have no fears, worries, hates and loneliness, you cannot be other than poised. You live each day with all the patience and poise of one who knows he is eternal and that nothing can change this. Each day can be a glorious adventure and can bring forth more good from the infinite and eternal treasury of Divine Mind.

But nothing can be taken away from your eternal nature, nor can you suffer any real defeat. No matter what the situation, you do not give in to any mortal weakening. If you catch yourself for the moment becoming upset, you quickly remember you are a spiritual being who is having Earthly experiences. You are truly in this world but not of it.

You radiate this poise to all about you and they become more poised. You have forgotten the time when you did not have this spiritual poise; the time never existed when you did not have it, you just did not know and act it. Your poise in every situation leads others to inquire how you attained it, and if they can also. This is one of the most effective ways of bringing one to one's own Self.

No matter what has been, you now and always act with perfect poise. You have complete Self-confidence. Nothing can happen that could in any way prevent your eternal unfoldment and enjoyment of life. All is well. Do you accept this gift of Self to self? Say so, act so, be so. "Thank You, Spirit of perfect and complete poise. So it always is with me."

18. BE LOVED

You always are loved by God. Divine love sees you as potentially perfect and all your apparent imperfections as only temporary mistakes on the way toward eventual manifestation of your inherent perfection. Others do not see you this way when they use only the outer vision. God has given us an inner vision. Use of this inner sight enables you to see yourself and others as God sees you: in the process of becoming perfect. There is no schedule for each one; it is an individual process, but all will attain in due season. God knows this, for He said so when He created man.

If you also will see all others, and yourself, in this same way, all as potential and eventually manifested perfect spiritual beings, you will see them with divine love. Both you and they will be blessed. You will be loved. Others may not know why, but they will be drawn to you. What you are doing is recognizing and greeting the Self within each one. The Self responds in love. All may not seem to return your love, but do not let that bother you. You know what they really are even if they do not. As you radiate love to each and every one, to all creation, love flows back to you. Yes, all the world does love a lover. Whatever others give to you, give them love. This also would lessen or eliminate harm others might attempt upon you.

"I am one with divine love. I send nothing less than love to others. I recognize and salute the spiritual Self in each one. I tell them so by name, even though it may be silently. I accept love from them when they are ready to give it. The more I give of Your love, dear God, the more I have to give and to enjoy. I do in reality thereby give Your love to You, for You are all there is. Thank You for this wondrous gift of eternal love."

19. BE ADMIRED, RESPECTED, LIKED, TRUSTED

You must give what you would like to receive. There is something to admire, to respect, to like and to trust in every person, no matter what the appearances are, for God is in every person. You need not approve of his improper actions, but remember that is how he is acting and not what he truly is. One who cannot see perfection within everyone and everything cannot achieve perfection himself. Nor does he see God truly, for God is within each person and is the manifesting form of everything. This does not mean every manifested thing, such as a disease organism, is desirable, but it does mean that Spirit is forming it. If it is not a desirable form, we have the power to have it changed.

To be admired, admire others. Whether it be entirely or for some particular characteristic, let them know. Look for something to admire and you will find it. Praise sincerely. To be respected, respect others. Deep within, every man, woman and child feels he or she is someone. So they are; each is an expresser of God. Respect them for what they are or are not, or for what they do or do not; there always should be respect for the divine presence, and It is in everyone. Show your respect. To be liked, like others. Like something they think or do; look for something to like. You may not like all they think or do, but like something. Let them know it.

To be trusted, trust others. One who basically does not trust others is not acting in a manner deserving of trust in him. One who distrusts others has no trust in God, regardless of what he says. Most people will live up to expressed trust in them. It is a wonderful stimulant to many. Those who would betray such trust will not harm you nearly so much as themselves. But you must express trust in order to be worthy of trust.

20. KNOW GOD EXISTS

Sincerely ask Him to reveal Himself. Do not be impatient. Do not try to tell Him how or when to do it. Only ask that you be made to know. Do not try to reason His existence. God is beyond the intellect and never can be found through it alone.

21. KNOW GOD

When you know God exists, you can begin to know Him. "In praise and humility, I ask to know You, dear God. I would know our relationship. I would know Your nature, Your power and Your purposes. I ask to be instructed by You, that I may know You as I should. Thank You."

22. KNOW YOURSELF

"I ask my Self within to teach me who and what I am. Please reveal our relationship. Show me what I should do to correct my faults. Instruct and guide me in all I do as I seek to know and to express my Self. Let me know my reason for being and what I am to do. Advise me in all my decisions. Lead me to oneness. So be it."

23. EXPRESS GOD

"I am one with Divine Mind. I am a center of consciousness of Divine Mind. I am one with all attributes of Divine Mind. I express these attributes perfectly. Divine love, abundance, peace, understanding, imagination, wisdom, joy and all other divine attributes are expressed fully through me. My consciousness expands to understand and to express more of Divine Mind. I learn how to use the powers of Divine Mind. I accomplish the purposes of Divine Mind. I express in Divine Mind and Divine Mind expresses in me. Divine Mind and I are eternally one. Thank You for this gift."

24. KNOW WHAT YOUR WORK IS

Ask Spirit to guide you to your proper work. Meanwhile, do well whatever good work you are doing now, be it working, studying, looking for work, recuperating or whatever else. Work in this sense does not mean just employment, but everything you do in life. Know that you have a work you can do which is needed. There are countless works to be done and workers are needed to do them: miners, scientists, farmers, typists, painters, factory workers, housewives and mothers, accountants, salesmen, janitors, musicians, metaphysicians and countless more. You could be one or many of these. There are many works to be done that as yet are not known generally.

Accept the strong suggestions given by Spirit. Know there is a proper work for you and that you always will be doing what you should. Sometimes you will be led to it and sometimes it will come to you; there are many ways in which Spirit accomplishes. Leave yourself open to all channels through which these works can come; do not attempt to say how they must arrive. Know you always will be doing the right work, and so it will be. Know you are of the utmost importance to God; there never has been or could be anyone just like you. Your work is needed. Ask Spirit to show you this work, then do it well.

25. HELP OTHERS

"In the morning, before arising, I ask You to guide me to help others in whatever way You wish. I look forward to doing whatever I can, for we are all equally part of You. I ask that I be given greater understanding so I may be of always greater help. Thank You for this opportunity, for I know I am helped as I help others. I am at Your disposal at all times, knowing You plan my work and time so I accomplish all I should. So be it."

26. SEE GOD

God is infinite Mind, and all there is. In the physical sense, infinity cannot be contained completely in the finite. However, each finite manifestation is part of, is composed of, infinite Mind. When Job said, "Yet in my flesh shall I see God," he meant that literally. Not in his physical body would he see God in His separate physical body, for it is not possible that God have only one finite body. But he would recognize his very flesh as being composed of God. This is the only way you possibly can see God in the physical sense: as every physical thing there is.

In the mental sense you can recognize God more fully. Infinite Mind is the Mind you use. The more a person realizes this, the more he is able to encompass infinity. In this manner can the infinite be expressed more and more fully through one's individual consciousness. In this way you mentally can see God as the innermost being of every person. The more you think of all persons and all physical manifestations in these two ways, the more you see and live with God.

The mental or intellectual eye cannot see or comprehend God fully. This requires the spiritual eye, which does not see physically or does not imagine mentally God, but knows Him. When you are able to know in this manner, you see that you are part of what you have sought. The mental and physical seeing then are found to be one with the spiritual knowing, and all seemingly individual parts are part of you. Then truly do you see God; there is nothing else to see.

27. CO-OPERATE WITH GOD

You, and all others, exist to manifest God. This does not mean as master and slave or as director and robot. It means exactly what it literally says: a manifestation of God. God and you are one to the extent you recognize and enact that oneness. When you think of God as separate and distinct from you, there is that separation only in your thinking; God is still one with you. When you are able to regard yourself both as one with God and as an individual personality expressing God, you are able to co-operate with God. In this co-operation you are a means whereby infinite Mind operates or performs actions in the finite or manifested world.

The Director made the stage and scenery and has a continuous story to produce. The set has been made by and of Him. The story is His. He next created the cast; He needed one in order to have the story unfold. The members of the cast also must be made of Him, since there is nothing else. To have action and to partake in the story, He became the animating force in each of the actors, as well as everything else. In this way He is able to maintain the set and its action. In this way also can He express in the story. But He did not create the manifestations as something separate from Him; He became part of them and they part of Him.

In order to do so and also to retain overall awareness and control of this drama, in addition to many others, He assigned part of His attributes and functions to each member of the cast. When these individual centers of consciousness first made their appearances, some thought they were separate members of the cast. Many sought to become stars and to own the stage and all the property on the set.

Gradually they came to realize they were not separate, limited actors but actually were part of the Director who was acting in each. Each found the Self within. The Director had known all along that He was in each. But in order to be part of the operation in the play on the stage, He also had to have awakened the consciousness of Self within each manifestation of Him. This alone could give Him full participation in His own creations.

In such manner is one able to look to the Self within his or her own consciousness and to learn what the plot is, what his part is and how to enact it. Then he turns back to the world and puts his part into operation. In addition to playing his role in the main story, he has ample time to participate in other actions and to enjoy living life in both the major and minor plays. He co-operates in the individual sense that he does not allow his thinking and action to be only in the finite. He co-operates, or operates together, Self and self; he is one.

"Dear God, I ask that You awaken my consciousness fully so I may know and then become my Self. May I truly learn the nature and meaning of co-operation with Divine Mind. Above all else I wish to know of this co-operation and how to achieve it. I ask that this knowledge be presented to me when I am able to receive it and that I know it as truth beyond any shadow of doubt. Guide and teach me so I may be able to receive this wisdom. So be it. Thank You."

28. ACT WITH OTHERS IN MAN'S PROGRESS

Much progress has been effected by competition. Far greater progress has been prevented by competition. Without dwelling on the waste of effort and money in attempting to share in the glory and material wealth of bringing forth any idea into manifestation, competition is a serious hindrance to the purpose of everyone and everything, which is the expressing of Divine Mind. There are many wondrous ideas in Divine Mind awaiting man's co-operation in bringing them into manifestation. Man would progress much faster if he would seek new ideas rather than embellish those already well manifested. Nor would this lack of competition mean lack of improvement in ideas.

When man learns he does not originate basic ideas for products but they already exist in Divine Mind, he will not see so often only part of an idea and, instead of waiting for the rest of the already perfect idea, try to complete it with limited understanding. Instead, he will ask God for an idea to manifest and will wait for the idea to be unfolded sufficiently before setting about to produce it. It is not necessary to try many fruitless experiments when one learns that the solution, if any, already exists in Divine Mind and all one need do is learn how to ask and to receive. Then instead of wasteful and hostile competition with others, there will come useful and loving cooperation between all. The whole cannot function smoothly and harmoniously when all of its parts do not work in cooperation.

If you are interested in converting any idea to its manifested counterpart, be it something already revealed or not, ask God for the complete idea. If you can understand it, bring it forth. If not, seek the help of others who can understand. Then, if it is not understood fully, do the best you can. But do not waste your efforts merely in trying to alter a minor part of an idea just to compete and to take away something from others. Co-operate with God and His express-ers and so bring forth divine treasures.

29. GET THE MOST FROM OTHERS

"I see all others as my potential equals." In reality no one is any more or any less than another in God's appraisal, although they are at different levels of spiritual evolution and expression. "Therefore, all have as much right to divine gifts as do I." Those who know this do not attempt to deny others their inherent rights. They do not at-tempt to benefit at the expense of others.

Those who do not know yet that all things in reality are God's, and therefore seek to take only for themselves, do so only because they do not know better. When they awaken to the truth that of themselves they own nothing, and yet own all things by being one with all, they no more will seek to deny the good of others.

"I ask Your prompting whenever I might make the mistake of harming anyone by in any way preventing him from obtaining any right thing in a proper manner. I would be careful that my personal wants never in any way cause lack or suffering for the innocent. I know in reality I gain nothing but lose much if I try to take advan-tage of others. I always get what I need and want through love and service, not force. I get the most good, in all ways, from others by giving my best to them. I am equally one with all others."

30. MAKE FRIENDS

To have a friend, you must be a friend. Sincerely try to make friends; there are many degrees of friendship. It is really a simple thing to enjoy friendships. All you need do is let yourself be friendly. There are many opportunities to contact people; many of these, in some manner, can be friends of yours. Ask Spirit to help you to develop friendliness so you can have friends. Take the initiative and see all you meet as friends, in some degree.

To the extent you are capable of being a friend, Spirit will lead you to those with whom you can be such. Be sincerely interested in and friendly to them and they will be interested in and friendly to you. Do not worry about any seeming inadequacies on your part, but just be natural. Spirit will initiate the contacts.

31. SOLVE ANY PROBLEM

Know there is a solution, no matter how impossible it may seem. Know that God, who knows all things, is aware of your problem. How? Because you use Divine Mind in thinking. Know that God, who is one with all creation, knows aspects of the problem from a far better vantage point than do you who are immersed in it. He can initiate actions through other persons and things that you, with limited human vision, cannot know about or cannot initiate. When you personally are involved in a problem, you cannot see more than a limited part of it because you view it as concerning only part of the whole.

Turn in thought to God and ask that the solution be made known to you. It makes no difference if it is your or another's personal problem, a problem of science, making a decision, or anything else. Nor does it matter if you caused the problem or not. Ask God for the solution, be sure you will receive it, give thanks that the solution is already on the way, and look for it. But you must ask; just knowing about it is not taking any action. So rather than wasting effort and becoming upset, ask God. He is always ready and anxious to help.

However, do not become so dependent that you fail to learn through these problems and their solutions. Remember you are interested in developing your spiritual awareness and ability to initiate action directly, not by continually asking God or another to do it for you. But do not seek to avoid it, for only by facing it can you solve it, if it is one that warrants solution. Naturally, this does not refer to the creation of imaginary problems just to test this principle. Even this has a solution, though: ignoring such nonsense. Meeting and solving problems, for all are not unpleasant, is a mark of your spiritual unfoldment.

32. FIND YOUR PROPER PLACE

You are now in the place where you belong, according to your thinking and action; lack of thinking and lack of action apply too. This may seem harsh judgment on some, but it is not a judgment at all. It means each is where he now is because of what he did or did not think or what he did or did not do. Not knowing what to think or to do has not altered the result; you still are where you are, and thus belong. If you do not like where you are or if you are willing to move into a greater expression of life, ask Spirit to instruct and to guide you.

The statement that you are always in the right place at the right time is misleading unless you differentiate between being where you belong, according to the previous explanation, and being at the proper place, as is explained next. When you have asked Spirit to be your divine guide and then apply yourself to learning and to using divine instructions, you always will be at the right or proper place at the right time.

"I place my affairs in Your care, dear God, and know You will guide me so I always will be in the right place at the right time. Wherever I am, I express You; therefore, I am always at my proper work. Let the will of my Self, and not my self, be done. Thank You for always granting this. So be it."

33. MAKE THE TRUE MARRIAGE

It is said that true marriages are arranged in heaven. That is always so. It is up to man to find and to complete that marriage in the world. But this applies to the divine marriage, the union of Self with self. These are the two who become one and dwell in one flesh. Not man and woman, but Self and self. They are not really two; man only thought so. The uniting is effected by recognition and proper action. The marriage of man and wife is a man-made combination, not a true spiritual union. Ask to know and to achieve this spiritual marriage.

34. DISCOVER PERSONAL TALENTS

Know that everyone is an expression of God. Divine Mind is the source of all talents. At any one time everyone could not express all talents. But everyone can discover, develop and express some talents. If you do not know as yet of any personal ability, ask Spirit to inform you. Feel that the expression of this talent gives Divine Mind an opportunity to manifest more fully for the benefit of all concerned.

Then watch for developments. Ideas will come to you mentally, physically or both. A number of apparent coincidental events or attractings of your attention may lead to your knowing the answer. When you do learn of a particular talent you can express, and it may be but one of many for you, develop it. Express your thanks by expressing the talent. There always are more awaiting you, too.

35. GUIDE ANOTHER

When someone asks for personal guidance from you, it is well that you give as you are qualified and able. This never means complete guidance in all things by you, whether asked for or not. Guidance by spiritual understanding is helping one with specific problems or with spiritual awakening and progress. It serves to help him help himself rather than always be helped. One always should be taught that his real guide is Spirit within him. You may be able to advise on some things, but only his real Self knows what is best for him. Let him know this, but do not dwell on it unless he seeks more information.

As for spiritual guidance of those who have not sought it, you have no right to interfere personally. But you can and should greet the Self within him and ask that he be guided by that Self in whatever way is best for him. See him expressing his Self. Many wondrous awakenings are made in this way. You have the power to call forth the Self in another, for you are at one with that Self. But you cannot decide for the other as to his recognition of and guidance by that Self. Be guided by Spirit yourself, also.

36. ACQUIRE KNOWLEDGE

Whatever you want to learn, realize it is known already by your Self. The attainment of knowledge is for the purpose of having conscious access to it when you want to use it. When you do this by conscious learning, you need no strenuous effort. Before you study, ask Spirit to impress it in your memory and to present it to your conscious attention when you have need of it. Or instruct your subconscious to retain and to divulge it in the same way. This will take practice, but it eventually will enable you to learn and to remember far more through conscious acquisition of knowledge.

The ultimate will be when you attain the understanding that since your Self already knows all things you need to be aware of, there is no need to acquire knowledge by laborious conscious study. The knowledge you want will be presented to your conscious attention as you desire or have need of it. This is part of knowing rather than thinking. Then you will see that thinking can be devoted to using, and is not needed for acquiring, knowledge. Much of the knowledge one gains on Earth consists of facts which never will be used. Therefore, it is wisdom not to devote too much time to learning facts one never will need. Wise is the one who seeks and acquires spiritual understanding, which will be useful at every time and place in eternal life.

"I ask that I be guided by You, Spirit of all wisdom, in all my eternal search for and acquisition of knowledge. May I be instructed by You in spiritual truth of realities that never change and which therefore will be of value to me forever. I ask You to help me determine what are changeable facts and what are eternal truths. The facts I use according to worldly value, while truth I use to expand my spiritual understanding and work. Thank You."

37. RELAX

Make yourself as comfortable as possible. Issue mental instructions to your consciousness that your thinking and body are to relax. Decree that no thoughts except relaxing ones now have any place in your conscious thinking. Instruct your body to relax all tensed muscles; it knows how to do this. Let go your thinking and relax. Do not try to tell your body how to relax, step by step. Do not try to force your thinking to be restful. All such actions keep you working and tensed, hindering your relaxation.

When you have mastered this simple technique of letting your body relax in its own way and of forbidding anything but peaceful thoughts to enter your thinking, you will be able to relax at any time in only several minutes. As you progress in your spiritual training of thinking properly, you will find less necessity to enforce relaxation.

Meanwhile, master this simple relaxation method: "I have made my body comfortable. I am relaxing in thinking and in body. I request that my body now be relaxed completely. I enjoy the feeling as all unnecessary tension ceases. I delight in the looseness. All thoughts not of peaceful nature are forbidden to enter my thinking as I relax. I turn in thought to the spiritual realm of eternal peace. I am at one with that peace."

38. SLEEP WELL

Normally the cause of sleeplessness is inability to stop conscious thinking. "Peace, be still." This is one of the most powerful decrees, in many ways, when it is understood. In its use to stop unwanted thoughts from racing through your consciousness, you must know that your conscious will is the master of your mortal self. When you know your mastery and exercise it with authority, you can stop unwanted thoughts from remaining in, or even entering into, your consciousness.

The foregoing how-to on relaxing is a good beginning to deep sleep. The last part of the example given there is holding the word *peace* in your thoughts. Do not try to think of peaceful things but just the idea of peace. Peaceful thoughts will come, leading you soon to sleep. The important thing is your initial authoritative decree that all unwanted thoughts must cease immediately, then all conscious thoughts are to cease and you are to sleep. It is necessary to have your conscious thinking cleared before sleeping so you will not have a troubled sleep due to subconscious mulling of your waking thoughts. The best thoughts to hold just before sleeping are instructions to your subconscious for some constructive work on your body or thinking.

"I am about to enter a restful sleep. I request that my body be relaxed fully. I do not wish to have any more thoughts presented to my consciousness now. All is peaceful, and remains so throughout my sleep. During this sleep I ask my thoroughly competent subconscious to re-create my body according to the perfect spiritual pattern (or to provide the answer to some problem). Thank You. Now I sleep."

39. AWAKE ENTHUSIASTICALLY

Of course, one necessary prerequisite is a restful sleep. But it takes much more than that. It requires a desire to be up and about another day of wonderful living. Make this desire for an enthusiastic awakening one of your last requests before entering sleep.

"I visualize my enthusiastic awakening after this sleep. Fully rested, I will be eager to be up and about another joyous adventure in God's eternal paradise. No matter how appearances may seem now, I am confident You have prepared wonderful growth and experiences for me for the day. Thank You. So be it."

40. CONDITION YOURSELF FOR PHYSICAL WORK

You can prevent undue body strain and fatigue, as well as make all physical effort much easier, by understanding what makes your body move and by paying special attention before beginning a particular effort that is strenuous. In general, you will find physical work far easier when you understand that Spirit, not you, does the work. Most fatigue comes from believing you are doing the work. Your thinking this causes your subconscious to manifest fatigue in your body according to your mental commands or expectations. When you know that Spirit actually does the work, you let Spirit operate your body in the proper manner.

Also of importance in such recognition is that a belief you should feel the strain is not to be issued as a thought to be manifested. Finally, Spirit is able to bring much more force into direct operation on the work if your own thinking does not interfere, thereby using some of this force against yourself.

In particular situations of physical effort which ordinarily might result in painful aftereffects, especially when you are not used to such efforts, you can tell your subconscious that, since Spirit is going to be doing the work, your body functions perfectly with no strain and with no abnormal inharmony. Those whose work is largely physical, those who do only occasional physical work, and athletes can benefit greatly from recognizing Spirit as the moving power of the body and asking to function in perfect harmony with Spirit in their work or sport.

"I am one with the only power there is. I recognize You, Spirit, as the moving force in my body in all its physical work. I decree that my body always work in full accord with Your power, thus enabling it to do far more with much less strain. In particular tasks, I know Your power is sufficient to do the work without strenuous effort and there will be no ill effects. Thank You for this work and excellent body condition. So be it."

41. STOP UNWANTED HABITS

Easily and quickly you can stop any and all unwanted habits, provided you really want to. Or if you only want to break the apparent hold of a habit without stopping it entirely, you can do that too. If you cannot do so by yourself, stop trying to do it by sheer willpower. That usually tends to make the habit stronger because you are adding strength to it by emphatic recognition of it as something you cannot control; you give power to what you really want to deny power. Use the denial and affirmation method of controlling or eliminating it.

"I hereby deny this desire any power to dictate to me. I am master of what I want, and this includes body needs. I decree that I have no further desire for or need of this practice. My word is law unto that which I speak, and must be obeyed. Neither my thinking nor my body henceforth will want this practice. I am free. So be it."

If as yet you have not reached this ability to command, you may ask Spirit to do it and it will be done. As you progress you will find such changes taking place with no conscious initiative or effort whatever. You suddenly have no more desire for what in any way is not harmonious with your developing spiritual nature.

42. LOCATE SOMETHING

If it is something new you want to locate, such as a job, house, person or any other particular item, all you need do is ask Spirit to bring you together, meanwhile doing what you normally would in such a search. If it is not necessary that you have one thing in particular, do not specify too exactly. Allow Spirit to bring that or something better. If you are searching for something you are not able to find, know that nothing is ever lost in Divine Mind. You are the one who does not know where it is. Tell Spirit what it is you wish to locate and give thanks that you now are made aware of its location, or that it is on its way back to you.

43. FACE COMING EVENTS

Whatever the appearance of a coming event, it can be met with confident understanding that all will be well. This is achieved by knowing Spirit goes ahead to arrange for the situation to work out in divine order and harmony. If you lack courage or confidence to face it, let Spirit supply you. Always see the event as going well, in the best interests of all concerned. Remember that Spirit has no favorites; all are loved equally.

In looking ahead to the successful completion of a plan or a situation, you must see the result as already favorably established in the spiritual realm. When it thus has been established properly, each step leading to that result must be the right one, since the outcome already is specified, generally or particularly; unless the request is changed, such as by doubt or deliberate errors along the way.

"I look forward with the utmost confidence that You, Spirit which is all, go ahead and prepare the way in the best interests of all concerned. I decree the desired result already established; therefore, all steps leading to that result must be favorable to it. I am guided by You in all my actions leading to this successful completion. So be it. Thank You for this and other things You are and do."

148

44. OVERCOME UNHAPPINESS AND GRIEF

God is all there is. No matter how unpleasant things may seem or how unhappy or grief-ridden you may be, it is only a temporary condition in your eternal life. All unpleasantness and unhappiness will pass away; much sooner, if you will permit. God is life, always seeking to express more fully through you. Give up sadness and accept the pleasures and happiness God has for you.

Become your Self and experience spiritual peace and joy. Command yourself to forget sadness and ask God to express joy through you. Ask that all of your senses and thoughts be considered at His disposal so He may experience and enjoy the full expression of joyous living through you. You need not attempt to decide what these coming pleasures and joys shall be or how they should come. Just live each day with the feeling that God is seeing and otherwise experiencing everything you see and do. Life must live, and you are part of life. Live. So it will be.

45. STOP PAIN

In your nervous system, pain is the signal that your conscious attention is wanted to some past, present or future happening in your body. It may be something: you are doing wrong, being done to you or not functioning properly. Once your attention has been attracted and you have set about to remedy the situation, there is no further need for the pain signal. You have it within your power to establish a decree that pain no longer be felt once it has served its purpose.

This law should be established now and repeated occasionally so it will be a part of your subconscious operating pattern before you have need of it. When you do need it, for yourself or others, it will be much easier to stop any pain. As you progress you will have less, and eventually no, pain as your body corrects all imperfections and maintains itself and its functioning properly. The protection caused by your conscious expression of divine love will prevent any serious injury, and you will not be committing serious foolish offenses against your body.

In treating others as well as yourself to stop pain, it may be necessary to take attention away from pain long enough, sometimes only seconds, for your decree to take effect. This can be done by remembering how it was before, when no pain was felt.

46. THINK POSITIVELY

Do not think negatively. It is not possible to think consciously in both a positive and a negative manner about the same thing at the same time. Perhaps in the beginning you have to force yourself, sometimes with great effort, to put away negative thoughts. But it always can be done; if not by you, then by Spirit at your request.

As you deliberately train yourself to think positively, your subconscious pattern of thought becomes positive. Much sooner than you now may imagine, you will have few occasions for deliberate putting away of negative and holding of positive thoughts; you will be thinking positively always.

47. MANIFEST ABUNDANT SUPPLY

It is most unfortunate that poverty has been preached to man as a spiritual trait. This is a deadly teaching that has caused untold suffering, both directly and indirectly. Whether it has been taught deliberately or unintentionally, still it is deadly because of the great damage and limitations it has caused. This strong language is used to emphasize the extent of the poverty error.

There is only one God; He is infinite abundance. If there were only a few stars, planets, people, trees, plants, animals, drops of water, grains of sand, atoms or any divine manifestation, then we could point to an impoverished god and teach that man too, made in this god's image and likeness, must be poor. Since this is not so, and never could be, we must teach the truth about supply.

God is infinite wealth and constantly is expressing abundance of substance, while manifesting more. It is our purpose in life to express God. We certainly are not expressing Him properly when we are poor.

The true intent of such spiritual teachings is that one must not devote his time primarily to the pursuit, possession and enjoyment of material wealth. True wealth is spiritual, from which come all ideas and which is all manifestation. It is not meant that one should concentrate primarily on obtaining a certain amount of material wealth before beginning to obtain wealth in spiritual understanding. "But seek first the kingdom of God, and His righteousness; and all these things shall be added unto you." Nor does this mean to forsake abundant material supply until you have achieved spiritually.

The dangers in material wealth lie in too much concentration on it, to the exclusion or limiting of the real things of life and the inability to give it up easily when necessary. You must relinquish all material possessions when you pass from your present life to the next one. But it is part of the full expression of life to use and to enjoy the abundance God has created for your use. All sensible use of this wealth, not just that which is channeled through religious and charitable organizations, is for divine purposes.

The terrible effects of preaching poverty can be seen throughout the world, especially in those countries where the people really believe and practice it. Poverty thinking has become so entrenched in race thought that much must be done to erase it from the subconscious thought patterns, even among those who think they have eliminated the poverty consciousness. Let this discussion also serve to cancel the poverty belief in all persons. Having no place in reality, it is denied any place in man's consciousness. So be it.

"I am one with God. You are the God of infinite abundance. There never can be any lack of You in Your kingdom. I am one with You and therefore one with all Your kingdom. I am created in Your image and likeness and I so express. I realize Your kingdom consists of what we call the spiritual, mental and physical realms; although they are in reality but phases of the one kingdom.

"I am provided abundantly with Your wealth in all realms. From Your spiritual treasury I take priceless spiritual riches, which I apply in the mental and physical realms. These spiritual treasures are Your ideas, which I combine with the mental riches I possess and the physical wealth You have provided as my body and all physical manifestations. In this manner do I achieve the kingdom of heaven and have all Your gifts added unto me.

151

"I realize that only as I give do I truly receive and enjoy Your gifts. Your manifested abundance of wealth is to use, not to hoard. I see myself as an expresser of infinite abundance. I preach the proper use of infinite abundance, and I practice what I preach. I am now fully open and receptive to Your gifts in all realms. I declare this for my entire consciousness, superseding any previously held thought to the contrary. So be it forever. Thank You for You as all this and far more."

48. BE ATTRACTIVE

To be attractive in appearance and manner, all you have to do is think and act in a spiritual manner. Consciously radiate divine love and other divine attributes along with your own blessings. The body manifests the way of thinking and acting. You cannot be other than radiantly attractive when you think and act in your divine nature.

49. STOP ANNOYANCES

The only way to stop having things annoy you is to stop being annoyed at people, things and events. Often the person who annoyed you is not aware you are annoyed, or does not care, and certainly no thing or event can know of your annoyance. Usually the one who is annoyed is the one affected most; and also usually the one who has to put an end to such feelings. Many annoyances are due to another's thoughtlessness or indifference, deliberate or otherwise, but many are due to one's own impatience or wounded self-indulgent thoughts and actions.

Whatever the cause, you can rise above being punished by such allowing of things to annoy you. Instead of a frown and a bitter thought of destructive dislike, send the other a smile and a blessing of constructive love. You will have given something positive, and you will be strengthened by the harmony within rather than weakened by inner turmoil. The other person may need your constructive blessing; although not perceived consciously, it may lead to more thoughtfulness on his part. Remember that you cannot be annoyed for long unless you permit it, so make certain the incident is worth upsetting yourself.

50. ALWAYS BE RIGHT

Let Spirit be your guide in all things and at all times. It takes considerable desire and study to reach this goal. But do not mind the innocent mistakes you make while learning. They will not be held against you by God, and should not be by you. Do the best you know how while seeking to do better. This is all that is asked of you.

Being right also means doing right; action is a vital part of being. When you can do things right, learn to do them better; doing something right does not mean necessarily doing it best. Be right in all things and do all things well. Be with God and do all things with Spirit.

▲

IV. HOW TO PRAY

Prayer in the proper manner is most important, because it invokes the power of the Lord God, which dwells equally in each. Some are not sure they pray aright. Some are not sure their prayers are heard. Some pray and find no answer to their prayers. Let us begin then from the very beginning, since we are about the most important business for Earth that we ever have embarked upon before. Because this shall take the efforts of the multitudes in concerted action, we speak now of the most essential and primary effort men can make together.

Prayer is the essence of all knowledge and humility that we are but instruments of the Divine. All know, who seek prayer and use it, that we are but humble agents of a much greater power than our own. But because we recognize that we are part of that power, we find it essential to invoke it and to bring it into focus where we are, and through us to speak the word that the Almighty Power, Father-Mother God can set it right. I now ask that all those who are in the spiritual consciousness begin to realize that their prayers are requested, that their prayers are needed and that their prayers need to be effective.

We still know that, before we ask, the Father within is already conscious of the need. So why ask at all? It is because we are connected with that power and are part of that power and seek that power to express through us that it is absolutely necessary that we deliver the request on the plane where we reside. This is essentially the reason why we must be projected into the Earth plane consciousness and have physical embodiment during this particular time.

If it were not required to have a physical outlet on a physical planet when a physical change was required, there would be no need of the light forces to be there during this very tremendous changeover from third to fourth dimensional frequency. Since it is essential to have powerhouses and broadcasting units of light in the form of the sons of God wherever the focus must be concentrated upon, we then have taken upon ourselves this duty and function as embodied forces of that light and of that power through vehicles and personalities; in fact, our souls are incarnated upon the Earth, as you know it.

Then instead of seeking our personal will as to what is necessary for this change and bringing about this change in the manner that we see fit, first we ask of the Father within what must be done. Since we know, each one who is in the light, that the same Father or Spirit resides in each other one, we seek that will and the way of that Spirit which is echoing Itself through Its multitudinous, infinite variety of expressions, the souls of men. So, humbly but forcefully, sincerely but with great understanding, we seek the Father's will in us and speak in His name first; that we invoke that Spirit who is residing in all forms equally and at the same time; to do Its bidding and to follow Its will and to express in the way that is best for everyone.

So, before the prayer is formed in one's own mind, before we set about to change that which already is in manifestation, we call upon the Father, the will, the power, the truth, the light as It is in eternal existence, and can never be changed. Once we recognize this and once we recognize that this same force is in the condition that we think needs to be changed, we are set free from our own individual will.

We step aside from the desire that we think is so essential and let flow through our minds and hearts and total being the idea that is in divine will and consciousness. If nothing is said, if nothing is forthcoming, then that is the answer to our prayer. If some specific word is formed in our minds, some specific deed is desired, then it shall be revealed unto the receptive instrument who must perform the deed. This is truly how all in spiritual consciousness do work.

When all gather together in the Hierarchal Board, none is assured of what the job will be or who will be required to perform it. But since we come in equal consciousness of desiring the will of God and wishing to express it, regardless of the task and difficulties or the sacrifices individually, it is revealed; and revealed equally unto each one. It is this way that we know we are one and that we share the

155

same common Fatherhood and Motherhood of the spiritual Self and the spiritual energy that is in all and expresses through the Sonship or Christ Self.

What we are requiring, therefore, by giving this example unto you of Earth is that you seek to do the same things in like measure. For I tell you, in all truth and in all honesty, that what is to be required of sons of light upon the planet in the next forty years of time, as you count such time, will be this type of activity in concerted action: workers all together seeing and being the one truth, finding the one answer, being the beacons to force the light through the transmuting energies of Earth and all life upon the Earth. These are the duties of the sons of light in this particular dimension at this particular time and for this particular purpose.

In the days ahead many will call upon the light workers to focus their needs and their desires in eternal action and in spiritual, merciful thoughts. It will be because of this great need to teach and to demonstrate proper prayer and proper expression of the light that dwells within that we give this preliminary exercise to you. It is not because you have not this knowledge within but because it is absolutely essential that you understand it from the highest of demonstrations and from the experiences of those masters and teachers who guide and lead this planet into its proper position in the hierarchal scheme of things. You will be required to work in all forms of the Earth's evolvement, in one way or another.

Your call will be heard provided you put the proper emphasis on it. Your emphasis will be that which God, within all equally, desires; and when you yourself have purified your minds and hearts to the point where you have no set, preconceived notion or idea as to what must take place. For if you present yourself or your prayer request to the Father God in the manner of which you desire to see done, the effect will be limited. It will be limited according to the proper approach that you have made toward this. It will be limited because you are limited and colored and distorted in your request.

The next step, that is so important, is the amplification of souls who make the request or set forth to do this work. Where one or more are gathered in the name of Spirit, there Spirit is. It is so decreed and stated. This has multiple meanings, of course. First of all, it means your own inner Self will be where you are gathered in divine and impersonal will and emotional content. The conscious and subconscious areas of evolvement within you are as one, and then invoke the higher consciousness, which is the spirit that works through the vessel in this trinity aspect of man, which is a manifested form of the Trinity aspect of the spiritual Maker of life force itself.

But the gathering of two or more in the name of Spirit also refers to those who can be equal and impersonal and detached and in love with the same principle; individualized souls who will give of themselves and will give to each other equally and totally that which is desired by the Spirit. Through these individualized souls the Spirit can and will work in amplified form. It exercises Itself twicefold, threefold, fourfold, or according to how many are there and according to the level of the dedication and according to the purity of those who are present.

Let us take this example for one single moment. You may have two or four souls gathered who are purified, cleansed and totally dedicated. This amplification goes out four times to that request, where there are four gathered in the same idea or form of an idea. Add another soul to this who will come, participating in this not purified, not totally dedicated and distilling some other, lesser energy into the force field or focus of light. This does not amplify the group consciousness. This in some ways does diminish its effectiveness, because it bends or eliminates the line of concentration as it reaches out into the ethers to be recorded and returned unto the place that is needed or requested for change.

So, we see why it is so essential to include those in our focus points and in our joint efforts of equal consciousness, of equal dedication and of single-mindedness of purpose. This does not mean there is not to be joint effort of many who have yet to complete the work of self-purification and self-analysis. But it does mean one must realize as he adds to his own force field or group that only those who are of like mind and of like dedication can really amplify that which is requested.

We give this small example and in this small number and way only to assure you that because there is not the purification of motive and inner Self-realization, we have not seen the results upon the planet that are desired to be created in the times ahead. When the program unfolds to a much greater degree, you will see the wisdom of these words and of these instructions. You will see the application of them for the next forty years; because it will take that, at least a minimum of that, to bring about the many changes that shall be wrought upon the Earth planet and all life that resides on the Earth planet.

I give this only in a symbolic term of forty years of completion, although it is quite evident it shall be at least that length of time, if not more, to complete many of the works. This has nothing to do with other instructions as to the bulk of the program we have discussed as far as the immediate cleansing, purification and understanding are concerned. What we are discussing here are the prayers and the concerted efforts of light workers, purified and lifted into Christ consciousness, who will bring about the magnificent changes that are required of the Earth and all life form upon the Earth in the coming Golden Age.

Last but not least, we must speak of the effectiveness of these prayers. The prayer will be effective only if the workers and the broadcasting units of light remain firmly entrenched in the vision of that which they expect to see done. In other words, you may not waver from your expectation once the prayer has been set into motion. You must hold steady and fast to that which you are expecting to see manifested.

Only because you do know that the light is, and the light already has informed you of what it expects to manifest, and you allow the light to flow through you with this vision and purpose and amplify it with a number of similar broadcasting units of light can you then hold that image. To the extent you hold it, that is how quickly and how fully it shall manifest where and how it must be done.

These same applications will apply individually to specific cases where they influence a small number of people or situations, and it applies equally as well to very large situations where there will be many involved and affected by the changes or the desires for upliftment.

Let us then see what our next immediate step, what our next immediate function, is to be. We must realize that we have to gather together all those who will be of similar mind and similar heart and similar purification in order to request of Spirit those instructions from within to bring about upon the planet and through the people on the planet the desired expression.

When this is done, the call that is made must be made with every intention of Spirit's will and way being made manifest in that, rather than any individualized, personal, preferred route or happenstance. Let it then be one of undivided attention, one that will not deviate from the projected image that is set forth. This is the only way it can work. So, when you make your call, start at the beginning and work through each step as best you can so you do not diminish the effectiveness and do not delay the manifestation.

— El Morya, channeled via Nada-Yolanda; September 26, 1968

▲

It is sincerely hoped this book has been of assistance in your spiritual development and action. Many have read it numerous times over the years, each time discovering something else to work on or having a higher revelation from the high Self.

Mark-Age is interested in hearing of your spiritual awakening, development, experiences, goals, and desires to participate in the hierarchal plan and program explained in our literature. You may receive a personal response to your correspondence; but even if you do not, you will have our personal attention and spiritual response.

For a listing of Mark-Age books, booklets, courses, audio and video recordings, and subscriptions, please send for our free catalog.

GLOSSARY

NAMES AND NEW AGE TERMS

Abel: son of Adam and Eve, in biblical allegory; was not a person. Abel and Cain were the two clans of the Adamic race within the Elder race on Earth prior to Lemuria. The Abels wished to help raise their fallen brothers of the human subrace back into the fourth dimension. The Cains wanted to keep the humans in the third dimension as subjects.

akashic record: soul history of an individual, a race, a heavenly body.

Allah-Lu: a title similar to Christ, in another realm of this solar system. *L* is symbol of Elder race. *L* also symbolizes the descent from the spiritual to the Earth plane level. *U* symbolizes lifting from Earth plane of both negative and positive energies back up to the Divine Source.

angel: a being of celestial realms. Angels manage, direct and cocreate with God the forms that exist in all space and eternity. They are a separate kingdom from man, and cannot incarnate physically.

Aquarian Age: period of approximately two thousand years following the Piscean Age, beginning around A.D. 2000. Cycle during which the solar system moves through the area of cosmic space known as Aquarius.

archangel: head of a ray of life in this solar system. First: Michael. Second: Jophiel. Third: Chamuel (replaced Lucifer). Fourth: Gabriel. Fifth: Raphael. Sixth: Zadkiel. Seventh: Uriel (only one of feminine polarity).

Armageddon: the Latter-Day, cleansing, harvest, Mark Age period immediately prior to the Second Coming of Sananda as Christ Jesus. The era wherein man must eliminate the negativity in himself and the world.

ascended master: one who has reached the Christ level and who has translated his or her physical body into the light body or etheric body.

ascension: spiritual initiation and achievement wherein one translates the physical body into a higher dimension.

Ashtar Command: group involved in interdimensional space phase of hierarchal plan and program.

Ashtar Gabriel: commander of Sananda's master ship #10, an etheric spacecraft of city size.

astral: pertaining to realms or planes between physical and etheric. Lower astral realms approximate Earth plane level of consciousness; higher astral realms approach etheric or Christ realms.

astral body: one of the seven bodies of man pertaining to Earth plane life. Appearance is similar to physical body. Upon transition called death it becomes the operative body for the consciousness, in the astral realms.

astral flight: a journey by the astral or soul body.

Atlantis: civilization springing from Lemuria, dating from 206,000 to 10,000 years ago. Land area was from present eastern USA and the Caribbean to western Europe, but not all one land mass. Sinking of Atlantis was from 26,000 to 10,000 years ago; allegory of Noah and the Flood.

aura: the force field around a person or an object. Contains information graphically revealed in color to those able to see with spiritual vision.

auric: pertaining to the aura.

automatic writing: a channeled communication by one from another realm written via control of the subconscious of the channel over the hands. May be handwritten or typewritten. Paintings or drawings can be done via such automatic process.

beam, electromagnetic: used by space visitors, via their equipment, to effect control over person or thing on Earth.

bilocation: being in more than one place at the same time.

Cain: son of Adam and Eve, in biblical allegory; was not a person. See *Abel.*

cause and effect, law of: as you sow, so shall you reap.

chakra: a center of energy focus, located around one of the seven major endocrine glands, but which penetrates the other, more subtle, bodies.

channel: a person who is used to transmit communications, energies, thoughts, deeds by either Spirit or an agent of Spirit. Also called prophet, sensitive, recorder, medium, instrument.

channel, communications: one who is able to relay messages from this and higher planes or realms.

chohans: directors of the Seven Rays of Life, under the archangels. First: El Morya. Second: Kut Humi. Third: Lanto. Fourth: Serapis Bey. Fifth: Hilarion. Sixth: St. Germain. Seventh: Sananda with Nada. As channeled through Yolanda numerous times.

Christ: a title indicating achievement of the spiritual consciousness of a son of God. Also refers to the entire race of man as and when operating in that level of consciousness.

Christ, anti-: one who does not accept brotherhood and equality of all men as sons of God.

Christ awareness: awareness of the Christ level within one's self and of the potential to achieve such.

Christ consciousness: achievement of some degree of understanding and use of spiritual powers and talents.

Christ Self: the superconscious, I Am, higher Self, oversoul level of consciousness.

clairvoyance: ability to see beyond the physical range of vision; seeing via the third eye. A spiritual talent.

conditioning: spiritual, mental and physical preparation of one's consciousness and bodies.

conscious mind: the mortal level of one's total consciousness; which is about one tenth of such total consciousness. Usually refers to the rational, thinking aspect in man.

consciousness, mass: collective consciousness of race of man on Earth, all planes or realms pertaining to Earth.

contact: a connection with someone else on this or another plane or level of existence.

coordination unit: designation and function of Mark-Age Unit, Coordination Unit #7 for the Hierarchal Board, pertaining to coordination of light workers and light groups on the Earth plane for the hierarchal plan and program.

Creative Energy: a designation for God or Spirit or Creative Force.

death: transition from physical life or expression on Earth to another realm, such as physical incarnation on some other planet or expression on astral or etheric realms.

dematerialize: change of rate of frequency vibration so as to disappear from third dimensional range of Earth plane sensing.

devas: those intelligent entities of the etheric planes who control the patterns for manifested form in the etheric, Earth and astral planes, under the direction of the angelic kingdom.

devic: one of the kingdoms of God's creation of entities. See *devas.*

dimension: a plane or realm of manifestation. A range of frequency vibration expression, such as third dimensional physical on Earth.

disease: condition of dis-ease or disharmony.

Divine Mind: God or Spirit; in reality the only mind that exists, man having a consciousness within this one mind.

Earth: this planet. When referring to the planet, Mark-Age uses a capital *E,* as it is the only name for this planet that we have been given through interdimensional communications via Yolanda.

Elder race: those sons of God who did not become entrapped in the third dimension as the human subrace.

elect: one who has been chosen by Spirit and the Hierarchal Board to participate in the hierarchal plan and program, and who had elected so to be chosen. One of the symbolic 144,000 demonstrators and teachers for this spiritual program.

elementals: those intelligent entities supervising the elements which comprise manifested form in the Earth and astral planes, under the direction of the devas for those forms.

El Morya Khan: Chohan of First Ray. Prince of Neptune. *El* denotes Spirit and the Elder race. *Morya* is a code scrambling of Om Ray. *Khan* is a Sanskrit term meaning *king.* No Earth incarnation since Atlantis (despite claims by others), until recent one as Mark Age or Charles Boyd Gentzel (1922–1981), a cofounder and a director of Mark-Age. Assigned now as leader of the light workers in the astral planes for the Second Coming.

elohim: one or more of the seven elohim in the Godhead, heading the Seven Rays of Life; creators of manifestation for Spirit.

emotional body: one of the seven bodies of man pertaining to Earth life. Does not in any way resemble the physical body, but has the connotation of a vehicle for expression.

ESP: elementary spiritual powers, the definition coined by Mark-Age in 1966 to supersede the limited and nonspiritual usual meaning as extrasensory perception.

etheric: the Christ realms. Interpenetrates the entire solar system, including the physical and the astral realms.

etheric body: one of the seven bodies of man pertaining to Earth life. Known more commonly as the light body, the electric body, the resurrected body, the ascended body. Resembles the physical body, but not necessarily of the same appearance. This body can be used by the Christ Self for full expression of Christ talents and powers.

evil: error or mistake, in spiritual or metaphysical usage.

eye, third: the spiritual sight or vision. Spiritual focus of light in center of forehead.

fall of man: sons of God becoming entrapped in the third or physical dimension of Earth from 206,000,000 to 26,000,000 years ago.

fast: in the spiritual sense, an elimination of error thoughts, ideas and actions. In the physical sense, limiting the amount and the variety of food intake.

Father-Mother God: indicates male-female or positive-negative principle and polarities of Spirit. Also, Father denotes action and ideation; Mother symbolizes receptive principles.

Father-Mother-Son: the Holy Trinity wherein Father is originator of idea for manifestation, Mother (Holy Spirit or Holy Ghost) brings forth the idea into manifestation, Son is the manifestation. Son also denotes the Christ or the race of mankind, universally.

Federation of Planets: coordination and cooperation of man on all planets of this solar system, except as yet man of physical and astral realms of Earth.

forces, negative: individuals, groups or forces not spiritually enlightened or oriented, but who think and act in antispiritual manners.

fourth dimension: in spiritual sense, the next phase of Earthman's evolution into Christ awareness and use of ESP, elementary spiritual powers. In physical sense, the next higher frequency vibration range into which Earth is being transmuted.

free will: man's divine heritage to make his own decisions. Pertains fully only to the Christ Self; and only in part and for a limited, although often lengthy, period to the mortal self or consciousness during the soul evolvement.

frequency vibration: a range of energy expressing as matter. Present Earth understanding and measurement, as in cycles per second, not applicable.

gift of tongues: thought transference, in actuality, via speaking of unknown languages.

Glo-Ria: spiritual name during Mark Age period for female counterpart or twin soul of El Morya. Now in etheric. Last Earth incarnation was as Gloria Lee Byrd (1926–1962), Hierarchal Board channel.

Golden Age or Era: the incoming New Age or Aquarian Age, taking effect fully with the return of Sananda early in the twenty-first century. It will be the age of greatest spiritual enlightenment in Earth's history.

guide: higher plane teacher for one still on the Earth plane.

Hannibal, Dr.: present etheric plane function of St. Germain as coordinator for Western Hemisphere in hierarchal program; from his mother ship, spacecraft #1235, in etheric orbit around Earth since 1960.

heaven: an attitude and an atmosphere of man's expression, wherever he is. No such specific place, as believed by some religions; except to denote the etheric realms.

hell: an attitude and an atmosphere of man's expression, wherever he is. No such specific place, as believed by some religions.

Hierarchal Board: the spiritual governing body of this solar system. Headquarters is on Saturn.

hierarchal plan and program: the 26,000-year program ending around A.D. 2000 wherein the Hierarchal Board has been lifting man of Earth into Christ awareness preparatory to the manifestation of spiritual government on Earth and the return of Earth to the Federation of Planets of this solar system.

Hierarchy, spiritual: the spiritual government of the solar system, from the Hierarchal Board down through the individual planetary departments.

hieronics: higher plane electromagnetic energies transmitted from interdimensional spacecraft to assist transmutation of individuals and groups.

human: those of the race of man who became entrapped in the third dimension on Earth, forming a subrace.

I Am: the Christ or high Self of each person. Yahweh (Jehovah), in the Old Testament. Atman or Brahman.

I Am Nation: spiritual government of, for and by the I Am Selves of all people on Earth, to be inaugurated officially by Sananda upon his Second Coming. Neither a religion nor a political government, it is the congregation of all souls dedicated, above any other allegiance, to God and to expressing the I Am Self. Regardless of race, gender, age, nationality, religion or esoteric-group affiliation, everyone is a potential I Am Nation citizen. On May 10, 1974, the Hierarchal Board commissioned Mark-Age to implant the prototype of the I Am Nation.

I am that I Am: each one's identification with his Christ or I Am Self: the mortal (I am) self is part of, and must cooperate with, the Christ Self.

incarnation: one lifetime of a soul; not always referring to an experience on Earth only.

instrument: a person who is a channel for Spirit or an agent of Spirit. Synonym for channel, medium, sensitive.

Jehovah; or Yahweh: biblical term for Christ or I Am Self.

Jesus of Nazareth: last Earth incarnation of Sananda. Christ Jesus, rather than Jesus Christ; for Christ is not a name but is a level of spiritual attainment which all mankind will reach and which many already have attained.

karma: that which befalls an individual because of prior thoughts and deeds, in this or former lifetimes. Can be good or bad, positive or negative.

karma, law of: otherwise known as law of cause and effect. What one sows, so shall he reap.

Karmic Board: that department of the spiritual Hierarchy which reviews and passes on each individual's soul or akashic record. Assigns or permits incarnations, lessons, roles, missions for everyone in this solar system.

karmic debt: that which one owes payment for, due to action in this or prior lifetimes. Must be paid off at some time in a spiritually proper manner.

Katoomi: Hierarchal Board name for Lord or Archangel Michael. Titular head, with Lord Maitreya, of Hierarchal Board. Archangel at head of First Ray.

kingdoms: celestial, man, animal, vegetable, mineral, devic. Denotes a category of divine creation. Evolution is only within the same kingdom, never through the various kingdoms. Transmigration—incarnation of an entity in different kingdoms—is an invalid theory.

Kut Humi: Chohan of Second Ray. Known as Master K. H. Earth incarnations have included those as Lao-Tze, Aristotle, John the Beloved, Francis of Assisi, Leonardo da Vinci, and William Shakespeare. Known also in an etheric aspect (not an incarnation) as Babaji.

language, universal sign: transmission of messages, commands, energies or stories through higher plane control of body movements, especially arms and hands, of a channel.

Lemuria: civilization dating from 26,000,000 to 10,000 years ago. Land area was from western USA out into Pacific Ocean. Final destruction was 10,000–13,000 years ago; allegory of Noah and the Flood.

levitation: lifting one's body off the ground by spiritual, or by higher plane equipment, means.

light: spiritual illumination; spiritual; etheric. Also, God as Light.

light body: fourth dimensional body of man; his etheric or Christ body; one of the seven bodies relating to Earth living; the resurrected or ascended body through which the Christ powers and talents can be demonstrated.

light worker: a spiritual worker in the hierarchal plan and program.

logos: a spiritual entity manifesting a stellar or a planetary body, such as a solar logos or a planetary logos.

Lord: God; laws of God; spiritual title for officeholder in Hierarchy; designation given to one who has mastered all laws of a specified realm.

Love God and Love One Another: the two laws which Christ Jesus gave unto man of Earth. The motto of the White Brotherhood, the light workers in this solar system.

Love In Action: the New Age teaching of action with high Self, action with love; the Mark-Age theme and motto.

Maitreya: counterpart of Lord Michael. Holds office of Christ for this solar system. Master teacher of Sananda. Name indicates function: mat-ray, or pattern for Christ expression. With Michael, is titular head of Hierarchal Board; Michael as power, Maitreya as love. He is of the race of man in the etheric realm.

Mark Age: designation of the Latter-Day period (1960–2000), when there are appearing signs of the times to demonstrate the ending of the old age. Also, designation for the Earth plane aspect of that hierarchal plan. Also, the spiritual name for El Morya in his incarnation on Earth as Charles Boyd Gentzel (1922–1981), cofounder of Mark-Age Unit.

Mark-Age: with the hyphen, designates the unit cofounded in 1960 by incarnated Hierarchal Board members El Morya (Charles Boyd Gentzel) and Nada (Yolanda of the Sun, or Pauline Sharpe). One of many focal points on Earth for the Hierarchal Board. Coordination Unit #7 and initial focus for externalization of the Hierarchal Board on Earth in the Latter Days. Mark-Age, Inc. is the legal vehicle for Mark-Age, filed in December 1961 and legally recognized March 27, 1962.

Mary the Mother: mother of Sananda in his incarnation as Jesus of Nazareth. Twin soul of Sananda. Her incarnations include: Zolanda, a high priestess in Atlantis; and King Solomon, son of David, in Old Testament. Known also by her hierarchal role as Sol-O-Man, symbolizing soul of man.

mass educational program: spiritual program to inform and to educate the world's population concerning the hierarchal plan and program of the Mark Age or Latter-Day period.

master: one who has mastered something. An ascended master is one who has achieved Christhood and has translated or has raised his or her physical body to the fourth dimension.

master ship #10: mother-ship spacecraft of city size which is Sananda's headquarters for the Second Coming program. Has been in etheric orbit around Earth since about 1885. Will be seen by those on Earth when time approaches for Sananda's return to Earth as Christ Jesus of Nazareth and as Sananda, Prince of Earth. Also known as Star of Bethlehem.

materialization: coupled with dematerialization. Mat and demat are a transmutation or translation from one frequency vibration to another, from one plane or realm to another. Translation of chemical, electronic and auric fields of an individual or an object.

meditation: spiritual contemplation to receive illumination, or to experience at-onement with Spirit or one's own Christ Self or another agent of Spirit, or to pray or to decree or to visualize desired results.

medium: a term for a communications channel; a sensitive; an instrument; a prophet (the preferred term in higher realms).

mental body: one of the seven bodies of man pertaining to Earth living. Does not look like a physical body.

metaphysics: spiritual meaning is the study of that which lies beyond the physical, of the basic spiritual laws of the universe, and the practical application thereof in daily life on Earth.

Miami, Florida: approximate site of spiritual capital and Temple of the Sun on Atlantis. One of the last spaceports on Atlantis to welcome man from other planets. Original location of Mark-Age Unit, from 1960 to 1980. Name spiritually significant: M-I-AM-I.

Michael: Archangel at head of First Ray. Known as Katoomi on Hierarchal Board. With Maitreya, titular head of solar system government, or spiritual Hierarchy.

miracle: a spiritual manifestation, or a work. There are no so-called miracles possible, in the sense of circumventing a divine law.

mortal consciousness: the awareness of a soul during Earth incarnation, prior to Christ consciousness.

mother ship: a spacecraft housing many occupants, smaller spacecraft and much equipment. Often of city size.

Nada: Co-Chohan, with Sananda, of Seventh Ray. Member of the Karmic Board of Hierarchal Board, responsible for guiding souls in the rectification of karma. She was high priestess of the Sun Temple in Atlantis. Known also as Yolanda of the Sun (her soul record), she incarnated on Earth as Pauline Sharpe (1925–2005), a cofounder and a director of Mark-Age with El Morya/Mark/Charles B. Gentzel. A conscious, mental-telepathic channel, beginning in 1958 she received thousands of interdimensional communications, which Mark-Age has published since 1960.

negative polarity: refers to the female principle in creation. The rest or passive nature, as complementing the positive or action polarity.

New Age: incoming Golden Age or Aquarian Age. Began entry about 1960.

Om; or Aum: a designation for God. Means power.

one hundred and forty-four thousand: the elect, the demonstrators and the teachers of Christ powers during the Latter Days. The number is literal, in that at least that number must so demonstrate to achieve the spiritual goal of lifting man into the fourth dimension, and symbolic, in that it does not preclude any number of additional ones from being included.

phenomena: manifestations which man of Earth considers abnormal demonstrations but which are according to spiritual laws.

physical body: one of the seven bodies of man for living on Earth. Has been expressing in third dimension, but is evolving into fourth dimension. The vehicle for mortal expression of the soul on Earth. The physical on other planets of our solar system expresses as high as the eighth dimension.

pineal: crown chakra or highest spiritual center in the body. When the pineal gland is opened and the spark between it and the pituitary (third-eye center) is ignited, Christ consciousness occurs.

Piscean Age: the period of approximately two thousand years now drawing to a close for Earth, to be followed by Aquarian Age. One of the zodiac signs designating a section of space through which the solar system travels around a central sun.

pituitary: the master gland for the physical body, spiritually known as the third eye. The kundalini fire must be raised to the pituitary center before the pineal can be united for awakening the soul to Christ consciousness.

plane: a realm, a dimension, a level of expression.

planes of action: kingdoms on Earth. First, mineral: fundamental matter or form. Second, vegetable: intelligence to grow. Third, animal: self-realization of continuity; and love, feeling, desire. Fourth, man: self-consciousness of identity and potential of his powers; fourth dimensional frequency in third dimensional form, or animal body.

positive polarity: the male or action focus, as complementing the negative or female or passive polarity.

prince: a spiritual office and title, such as Sananda being Prince of Love and Peace as Chohan of Seventh Ray, and Prince of Earth as spiritual ruler of this planet.

prophet: in addition to usual meaning, it is the term preferred by those of higher planes in referring to a communications channel.

psychic: refers to the powers of man focused through the solar plexus chakra or center. Not as high as the Christ powers.

purgatory: no such special place, but indicates the frame of mind or experiences of one not in the spiritual light and activity.

realm: plane, dimension, a level of expression.

reincarnation: taking on another incarnation, on any plane or planet, during one's eternal life.

St. Germain: Chohan of Sixth Ray. Present hierarchal function is as Dr. Hannibal, commander of etheric forces in Western Hemisphere. Previous Earth incarnations: Rama Tault; Matthias, replacement for Judas as disciple of Jesus; Apollonius of Tyana; Christopher Columbus; Count Rakoczy; and last, Francisco Marto, one of the three children of Fatima.

Sananda: Chohan of Seventh Ray. Prince or spiritual ruler of Earth. One of Council of Seven, highest ruling body of the solar system. Previous Earth incarnations: Christ Jesus of Nazareth, his last one; biblical Melchizedek, Moses and Elijah; Zarathustra; Gautama Buddha; Socrates, Greek philosopher; leader of Abels, in allegorical story of Cain and Abel; leader of Noahs, in allegorical story of Noah and the ark. Presently located in etheric realm, from whence he directs entire operation for upliftment of man and his own Second Coming; headquarters is master ship #10, in etheric orbit around Earth since about 1885.

Saturnian Council: Council of Seven, highest ruling body of the solar system. Headquarters is on planet Saturn.

Second Coming: refers to each coming into awareness of his or her own Christ Self, and the return of Sananda as Jesus of Nazareth to institute spiritual government on Earth early in the twenty-first century.

Self, high: Christ Self, I Am presence, superconscious, oversoul, Atman, Yahweh (Jehovah). The spiritual Self of each individual. Differentiated, in writing, from mortal self by use of capital *S* in Self.

self, mortal: the spiritually unawakened consciousness of Earthman.

sensitive: channel, prophet, instrument, medium. One who is sensitive to or aware of spiritual realms and occupants therein.

seven in a circle: symbol of Sananda and of Mark-Age Unit. Signifies completeness, wholeness and the step before spiritual manifestation. Indicates the seven steps of creation, the Seven Rays of Life, the seven major spiritual initiations.

Seven Rays of Life: the seven major groupings of aspects of God; the Seven Flames. First: will and power (blue). Second: intelligence and wisdom (yellow). Third: personal love and feeling (pink). Fourth: crystallization (colorless, crystal clear). Fifth: unity, integration, healing, balance (green). Sixth: transmutation, cleansing, purification (violet). Seventh: divine love, peace, rest (gold and white). As channeled numerous times by Yolanda.

sin: error, mistake.

sin, original: man's mistaken belief that he can have an existence away from or be separated from Spirit.

sleep, teaching in: all persons are given spiritual instruction during their sleep state. Many are taken on trips, in the astral body, to other planes or planets as part of such instruction. Many perform works or do teaching while in the sleep state, via the Christ Self consciousness.

Son of God: with capital *S* for Son, denotes the Christ body of all mankind, collectively. With small *s* for son, denotes an individual. All men are sons of God and eventually will come into that awareness, heritage, power and cocreativity with God.

Son, only begotten: refers to the entire Christ body, which includes all of mankind, and not just a single individual.

soul: the accumulation of an individual's experiences in his or her eternal living. A covering or a coat of protection, over which the individual spirit can and does rely for its manifestations.

soul mate: one with whom an individual has had close and favorable association in one or more lifetimes. Each person thus has had many soul mates, but does not incarnate with or come into contact with all of them during any one lifetime.

soul, twin: as an individual soul develops, it expresses in male and female embodiments. Eventually it will begin to gravitate toward either male or female for its expression in the Christ realms. While so developing, Spirit guides another soul toward the opposite polarity along the same path. Thus when one enters the Christ realm as a male polarity, there will be one of female polarity to complement and to supplement, with the same general background and abilities. Each person has a twin soul. But this term does not mean one soul was split, to gain experiences, and then eventually merges back into oneness. Twin souls are two separate individualities at all times.

Source: a term for God, sometimes called Divine Source.

sphere: planet, realm, plane, dimension, level of expression.

Spirit: God, Creative Energy, Creative Force, Divine Mind, Father-Mother God, Original Source.

spirit: the spiritual consciousness or Self of man.

spiritism: communication with those who have departed from the Earth plane. Term preferred by those in higher planes in place of *spiritualism.*

spiritual: term preferred over *religious* when referring to spiritual matters, as there are specific dogma and connotation attached to *religious.*

subconscious: one of the three phases of mind. Denotes the soul or record-keeper phase, which also performs the automatic and maintenance functions of the physical body. The relay phase between the superconscious and conscious aspects of one's total consciousness.

Summalt: etheric commander for Eastern Hemisphere in hierarchal program; from his mother ship, spacecraft #7423, in etheric orbit around Earth. In a prior incarnation was Peter, disciple of Jesus of Nazareth.

superconscious: the highest of the three aspects of individual consciousness, consisting also of conscious and subconscious aspects. The Christ, I Am, real, high Self. The real individual, which projects into embodiment via having created a physical body for such incarnation.

sword of truth: denotes the use of God's word and law to eliminate error, and to guide and to protect spiritual persons.

teacher, spiritual: one who teaches spiritual matters. May be on this or a higher plane.

teleportation: spiritual power enabling one to move from one location to another via dematerialization and materialization, without physical means. A Christ power. Symbol for this in Atlantis was dodo bird.

tests, spiritual: tests of one's spiritual progress and lessons learned, given by Spirit, by one's own Christ Self or by other spiritual teachers. Not temptings, which never are given anyone by any of the above guides.

third dimension: the frequency vibrational level in which Earth and all on it have been expressing physically for eons. Being transmuted into the fourth dimension, which was begun gradually by the mid-twentieth century for completion in centuries hence, but well into the process by the end of the twentieth. Does not refer to the three dimensions of length, width and height, but to a range of vibration.

thought form: an actual form beyond the third dimension, created by man's thoughts. Has substance in another plane and can take on limited powers and activities, based on the power man has instilled in it through his thoughts and beliefs.

thought temperature: the attitudes of an individual or a group concerning a certain topic.

trance: unconscious or semiconscious state wherein one allows the mortal consciousness, or at least the conscious aspect, to become inoperative. Many communications channels enter such in order to permit those on higher planes to speak or otherwise to manifest through the channel's physical body and abilities. A valid form of channelship, but not as highly evolved as the conscious channel, who does not give up conscious awareness during channeling.

transfiguration: a change of one's features, or of entire body, caused by overshadowing by one's Christ Self or by an ascended master.

transition: term denoting death of an individual on one plane so as to begin a new life on another plane. Also, general meaning of making a change.

transmutation: spiritually, refers to purifying one's mortal consciousness and body so as to permit rising into fourth dimension, physically and as concerns Christ consciousness.

trials: spiritual tests given one in evolution to see if lessons are learned or if obstacles can be overcome, as in training for a soul mission or any part thereof.

Trinity, Holy: Father-Mother-Son, Father-Holy Spirit-Son, Father-Holy Ghost-Son. The three aspects of God.

twenty-six-million-year cycle: a period of evolution for man in this solar system. The cycle since the final fall of man on Earth, during which the Elder race has been attempting to raise the human race that had become entrapped in the third dimension. Cycle ended about A.D. 2000.

twenty-six-thousand-year cycle: the period of time, since the beginning of the fall of Atlantis, in which man of Earth has been given the last opportunity in this solar system for reevolution into the fourth dimension. The duration of a hierarchal plan and program to raise man from the third dimension into true status as sons of God. Cycle ended about A.D. 2000.

two-hundred-and-six-million-year cycle: an evolutionary cycle for man involving graduation in and around the central sun from which we originated. The period during which man has experimented with life form on Earth in the third dimension. Cycle ended about A.D. 2000.

two-hundred-and-six-thousand-year cycle: withdrawal of Elder race from on Earth; decline of Lemuria. Cycle ended about A.D. 2000.

unit: a group of two or more performing hierarchal plan works.

vehicle: denotes a body for one's expression, such as the physical.

veil, seventh: final veil separating man from knowing his divine heritage and powers.

ventla: higher plane term for spaceship.

verification: proof; process of proving.

vessel: denotes a vehicle or body for expression, as the physical body.

vibrations: the frequency range in which something is expressing; not in terms of cycles per second, or any present Earth understanding and terminology. Also, the radiations emitted by an individual, able to be received consciously by one spiritually sensitive to such emanations.

White Brotherhood: the group of spiritual teachers, guides and masters who, having discovered God's truth and having learned to demonstrate spiritual powers, are guiding those who have not into that same level of Christ understanding. Pertains to this solar system. Is not a formal or organized group. Also called the White Lodge, Ascended Masters Council.

within: denotes going into one's own consciousness.

world, end of: denotes ending of third dimensional expression for Earth and all on it, physically, and entry into a higher level of frequency vibration, the fourth dimension. The end of the materially-minded world of man so as to begin spiritual understanding and evolvement. Does not mean end of the Earth, but only entering a higher dimension.

wrath of God: the reaction upon man of his negative or error action contrary to divine law. Does not mean personal anger or action of God against man.

Yolanda of the Sun: Earth incarnation of Nada as Pauline Sharpe (1925–2005), a cofounder and a director of Mark-Age. Was her name at height of her Atlantean development, when a high priestess of the Sun Temple, located near what is now Miami, Florida. Also known as Nona of the Temple of Love on the etheric realm of Venus.